PRAISE FOR *CREATIVITY AND COPYRIGHT*

"A must-read for those who create original work and want to understand the line between copyrighted material and what they create."

Mike Medavoy, film producer and former studio head, whose filmography ranges from *Rocky* to *Black Swan*

"*Creativity and Copyright* is the grail you will never find in film school. Although written with the writer in mind, I would easily argue it's also a must-know for filmmakers, producers, managers—a no-regrets resource that finally reveals the creative power to be unleashed by your own legal muscle."

Demetra J. MacBride, producer of *Mystery Train, Night on Earth, When Pigs Fly, Coffee and Cigarettes*, and *Dead Man*

"A handy, user-friendly book for screenwriters who are looking for immediate, precise answers to their most pressing questions."

Denise Mann, head of the UCLA School of Theater, Film and Television's Producers Program

"All aspiring and working screenwriters should keep this book next to their computers."

Daniel Bernardi, author of *Off the Page: Screenwriting in the Era of Media Convergence*

"Somehow Geiger and Suber make crystal clear a topic every writer struggles to understand. Put it on your bookshelf next to the dictionary and thesaurus; it could save you from heartbreak, broken friendships, and financial ruin. Oh, and it's also a great read."

Daniel Pyne, showrunner, screenwriter, and author

"Howard Suber is perhaps the most knowledgeable person on the planet when it comes to the intersection of creativity and commerce in the film business. For more than four decades, students have entered his classroom to see the secrets of screen magic revealed—not only how movies work, but why they affect us so deeply, and how we can apply those secrets to our own work. In this book he and attorney-screenwriter John Geiger have provided the most comprehensive and accessible guide to the legal realities and avoidable missteps in the business—as well as how not to get ripped off!"

Writer-director Robin Russin, coauthor of *Screenplay: Writing the Picture*

"I can't imagine anyone else approaching this material more capably or in such a reader-friendly manner."

Tom Nunan, producer of *Crash* and *The Illusionist*

Creativity and Copyright

Creativity and Copyright

Legal Essentials for Screenwriters and Creative Artists

JOHN L. GEIGER & HOWARD SUBER

UNIVERSITY OF CALIFORNIA PRESS

University of California Press, one of the most
distinguished university presses in the United States,
enriches lives around the world by advancing
scholarship in the humanities, social sciences, and
natural sciences. Its activities are supported by the
UC Press Foundation and by philanthropic
contributions from individuals and institutions. For
more information, visit www.ucpress.edu.

University of California Press
Oakland, California

Library of Congress Cataloging-in-Publication Data

Names: Geiger, John L., 1959– author. | Suber,
    Howard, 1937– author.
Title: Creativity and copyright : legal essentials for
    screenwriters and creative artists / John L. Geiger
    and Howard Suber.
Description: Oakland, California : University of
    California Press, 2019 | Includes bibliographical
    references and index. |
Identifiers: LCCN 2018048202 (print) |
    LCCN 2018051057 (ebook) | ISBN 9780520972742
    (Epub) | ISBN 9780520303522 (cloth : alk. paper) |
    ISBN 9780520303539 (pbk. : alk. paper)
Subjects: LCSH: Copyright—United States.
Classification: LCC KF2994 (ebook) |
    LCC KF2994 .G45 2019 (print) |
    DDC 346.7304/82—dc23
LC record available at https://lccn.loc.
    gov/2018048202

28 27 26 25 24 23 22 21 20 19
10 9 8 7 6 5 4 3 2 1

To Ana Sufuentes & Luca Marc Geiger,
my family eternal
—John

To the screenwriting, directing and
producing students I have known
during more than half a century of
teaching film and television at UCLA
—Howard

Contents

Acknowledgments

Creativity and Copyright found its way into print because of Steven Jenkins, development director of the University of California Press Foundation. Were this a movie, he'd be our executive producer.

We are grateful for the generous help and tireless efforts of the University of California Press team—acquisitions editor Raina Polivka, and her editorial assistants Elena Bellaart and Madison Wetzell; senior editor Emilia Thiuri; developmental editor Ann Donahue; and copy editor Jan Spauschus—in preparing this manuscript for publication and getting us to the final cut.

Before guidance from the UC Press team, the project benefited from manuscript review and publishing advice from our friends and colleagues Nathan Cole, Suzanne Curtis, Ken Lee, Cortez Smith, and Michael Wiese.

Book aesthetics have always been important to us. Our special thanks to friend and colleague Charles Bigelow for his erudite eye in advising on the look of the book.

This project benefited greatly from the kind and careful attention of each of these participants. Any errors or omissions are uniquely ours. And between the two of us, we blame the other guy.

Disclaimer

This book is designed to provide accurate and authoritative information regarding its subject matter, is based upon sources believed to be accurate and reliable, is intended to be current as of the time written, and is sold with the understanding that neither the publisher nor the authors are engaged in rendering legal or other professional services to the readers. If legal or other professional advice is required, readers should engage the appropriate advisor for their particular needs.

Introduction

For most of Western history, there was no copyright or other such intellectual property protection for artists, because there was no need for it.

If you were a painter, writer, dramatist, or other artist during the Renaissance, you were not part of an open market. Instead, you had a patron, who paid you once for a work that couldn't be reproduced. Then as now, making a living as an artist was hard. Even if you were lucky or talented enough to attract a patron, you received no further compensation, at least not for that particular work. If that seems like a bad deal, keep in mind that your patron had no expectation of receiving a payoff, or revenue stream, for his money. Your patron was a buyer, not an investor. He hadn't commissioned your work for commercial purposes. He couldn't have prints or calendars made to sell at the gallery gift shop.

Copyright became necessary for the first time in the age of mechanical reproduction. Mechanical reproduction of a work changed that work from being merely a possession to being an investment. The patron who commissioned your work and paid for it now often did so with the hope of making a profit by reproducing the work for a broader audience.

We have written *Creativity and Copyright* to serve as a guidebook for screenwriters and others looking to increase their likelihood of success as professional writers. Our overriding purpose is to increase your understanding of the relationships among business goals, legal issues, and creative freedom. In our experience, a balanced approach is most likely to result in a long-term career.

As a screenwriter, you will usually focus on your writing. Writing is obviously controlled by *creativity*. At other times, you will be selling. Selling is controlled by *copyright*. Hence, *Creativity and Copyright*.

Law books are rules driven. How-to books are results driven. This book is neither a law book nor a how-to book. Instead, it is a user-friendly hybrid intended above all to be useful. We believe that if you understand the basic principles governing what you and others can and cannot do in terms of copyright law, then you'll be less likely to ever need a lawyer.

You may be considering this book because you want to know what, in terms of copyright law, you can't do. But this book is just as concerned with making you aware of what you *can* do.

Although ours is a very different sort of project, we take our inspiration from Strunk and White's *The Elements of Style*. Like Strunk and White, we have written a concise book providing an overview of major concepts and important details related to the craft of screenwriting, whether you are at the beginning of your career or are an experienced hand.

The following are some of the many questions and issues we address:

What can others take from you?

What can you take from others?

You want to do a film about real people; what permissions do you need?

How can you safely collaborate with writers, producers, and others?

What protects your material when you are pitching?

Has your screenplay been infringed?

When should you get a lawyer?

Interestingly, the United States Constitution does not use the term "creativity" or "copyright." Rather, there is what Constitutional lawyers refer to as the Progress Clause. Like so much of the Constitution, the Progress Clause is really brief, rather broad, and somewhat ambiguous. It reads,

> Congress shall have the power . . . To promote *the Progress of Science and useful Arts*, by securing for limited Times to Authors and Inventors the exclusive Right to their respective Writings and Discoveries. [emphasis added][1]

"To promote . . . the arts" is not necessarily the same thing as promoting artists. Or the careers of artists.

That's where *Creativity and Copyright* comes in.

CHAPTER ONE

Free for the Taking

What You Can Steal from Others,
and What Others Can Steal from You

We believe that the [writer's] argument rests on a
misunderstanding of the nature of the protection
afforded by copyright law. It is well established
that, as a matter of law, certain forms of literary
expression are not protected against copying.
United States Supreme Court, *Berkic v.*
Crichton, 1985[1]

We are not merely being provocative when we use the
word "steal" in the title of this chapter. All too often,
"stealing" is what creators *feel* they'd be doing if they read
or see something somewhere and then use it themselves
without getting permission. Correspondingly, when someone else takes something of ours, too often we say,
"They've stolen my stuff!"

Copyright law is not simply limiting; it is also liberat-
ing. Writers often unnecessarily constrict their creativity,
thinking "I can't do that" because of copyright law. But
you are freer than you think.

WORKS IN THE PUBLIC DOMAIN

Perhaps the easiest way to understand public domain is to think of it as the opposite of copyright. Any work not protected by copyright is within what is referred to as the public domain. In this chapter, we discuss the major categories of public domain materials that are *free for the taking* by you:

Expired copyrights

Facts/nonfiction

News and history

Ideas

Scènes à faire

Fair use of copyrighted works

EXPIRED COPYRIGHTS

Copyright protection does not last forever. Instead, protection is granted for a limited time, as set by statute. When copyright protection expires, the work then falls into the public domain and becomes free for anyone and everyone to use.

For reference or a refresher on the rules of copyright, see appendix A, "Copyright Fundamentals."

We periodically see remakes of movies based on classic works of literature. That's partly because those classics have fallen into the public domain. Any work by a deceased author first published before 1923 is in the public domain and is free for the taking. And that's most of the works that literature professors would call "classics."

For example, here's a sampling of two classics we see repeatedly:

Romeo and Juliet (William Shakespeare, 1597)

1936—Leslie Howard (Romeo), Norma Shearer (Juliet), John Barrymore (Mercutio)

1954—Laurence Harvey (Romeo), Susan Shentall (Juliet), Flora Robson (Nurse)

1968—Leonard Whiting (Romeo), Olivia Hussey (Juliet), John McEnery (Mercutio)

1976—Christopher Neame (Romeo), Ann Hasson (Juliet), Laurence Payne (Capulet)

1996—Leonardo DiCaprio (Romeo), Claire Danes (Juliet)

2014—Orlando Bloom (Romeo), Condola Rashad (Juliet), Donté Bonner (Sampson)

Great Expectations (Charles Dickens, 1860)

1934—Henry Hull (Magwitch), Phillips Holmes (Pip), Jane Wyatt (Estrella)

1946—John Mills (Pip), Valerie Hobson (Estella), Tony Wager (Young Pip)

1974—Michael York (Pip), Sarah Miles (Estella), James Mason (Magwitch)

1998—Ethan Hawke (Pip), Gwyneth Paltrow (Estella), Hank Azaria (Walter Plane)

1999—Ioan Gruffudd (Pip), Justine Waddell (Estella), Charlotte Rampling (Miss Havisham)

2012—Toby Irvine (Young Pip), Ralph Fiennes (Magwitch), Jason Flemyng (Joe Gargery)

2013—Jack Ellis (Jaggers), Christopher Ellison
(Magwitch), Paula Wilcox (Miss Havisham)

All of these filmmakers have "stolen" from the original stories of Shakespeare or Dickens. The approaches and tonality may be different, but the underlying story is the same. That's because works by Shakespeare were never under copyright statutory protection, and works by Dickens have all fallen out of copyright protection.

Currently, the United States copyright protection period is from the date of creation through the life of the author plus another seventy years.

How do you know if a copyright has expired? For Shakespeare and Dickens and anyone else who published and passed away so long ago, you don't need to worry or even do the math.

But what about for more recent authors, for example, twentieth-century novelists? You need to do a copyright search. Find the date of original publication, and then determine what the copyright duration was under the law *at that time*. Then do the math. For more about the changes (i.e., increases) in the duration of copyright protection in the information age, see appendix A, "Copyright Fundamentals."

If you're really concerned, you could engage the services of a lawyer for an hour or so to do this analysis for you, and then have them give you a written opinion letter confirming that the work is no longer under copyright protection.

For more, see the section about the movie *Treasure Planet* in chapter 7, "Confessions of an Expert Witness."

FACTS/NONFICTION

Facts are in the public domain, and they are free for the taking. The world is full of facts, and we don't just mean physical properties. When was the last time you saw a mathematical equation with a copyright notice on it? That's because the equation is a fact (or at least the author claims it's a fact).

Works published by the United States government are in the public domain because they are expressly excluded from copyright protection.[2] The government is not in the business of writing fiction. (Individual politicians may very well be, but the institution as a whole is not!) Moreover, government writing is done using our tax money. We taxpayers—the public at large—are the patrons. Public patrons, public domain.

The federal government writes training manuals, informational pamphlets, and other such pragmatic nonfiction. And the government is the publisher of the transcripts from court proceedings (which, as you might imagine, can be very fertile ground for story material).

For storytelling purposes, the most useable facts typically are those involving real events and real people. Perhaps the two biggest categories of factual works are biography (true life) and news and history (true events).

Biography—and biopics—are discussed in chapter 2, "Clearance Required."

NEWS AND HISTORY

News is the factual reporting of *current* events. History is the factual reporting of *past* events.

We can hear you grumbling from here! You say, "But news is sensationalized to attract an audience, history is written by the winners, and there is 'fake news' all over the place." We don't want to delve into a philosophical discussion about the nature of facts; that is, the reporting of an event is tainted by the subjectivity of the reporter, and therefore calls into question whether there are any purely *true* facts. People have argued over these issues for at least 2,500 years and we don't expect we could resolve the debate.

For copyright purposes, a current or past event is free for the taking, no matter whose version you believe, and even if we don't have complete agreement on what the event is.

Even speculative ideas about history are, for copyright purposes, the same as historical facts.[3] That's because the speculation is presented *as if* it were history. When you speculate about history, what you conclude is not protectable. You can only protect how you say it. For more, see the section on *Amistad* in chapter 7, "Confessions of an Expert Witness."

Sometimes the writer wants people to believe they've uncovered the truth ("the facts") about an event. But the writer can't have it both ways—if the story is claimed to be factual, then it is in the public domain and free for the taking. For more, see the section on estoppel in chapter 5, "Copyright Infringement."

Coincidentally, in recent years we both have been consulted by different writers with this same problem: The writer pitches a project based upon a historical figure and a historical event to a major director. The director ultimately passes. But later, the writer learns that the director has committed to do a film *on the same specific historical event,* but the focus will be on a different character.

Something just doesn't seem right. Despite the "pass," it seems like that pitch was really in the chain of project development, especially if the director was not previously considering—or even aware of—the historical event.

But this is not a copyright issue. If anything, it comes under implied contract and idea theft. More about that in chapter 4, "Selling to Others and Implied-in-Fact Contracts." This is a strategic problem for the screenwriter as much as a legal one.

IDEAS: "FREE AS THE AIR"

Copyright law does not protect ideas. Indeed, the Copyright Act expressly rejects protection of ideas:

> In no case does copyright protection for an original work of authorship extend to any idea . . . regardless of the form in which it is described, explained, illustrated, or embodied in such work.[4]

Further, the courts have repeatedly echoed that "ideas are free as the air,"[5] so you simply cannot copyright an idea. But neither can you steal one.

In chapter 4, "Selling to Others," we discuss the concept of *idea theft.* This is somewhat of a misnomer, because the actionable wrong is not the so-called theft, but rather the violation of an express or implied contractual promise to compensate the writer for any ideas they pitch that are actually used. More about this later. But in the absence of a contract (i.e., you have an express non-disclosure agreement or you're in a pitch meeting or other business context that suggests an implied contract), then your ideas are indeed free for the taking under the Copyright Act.

But What Is an Idea?

It is commonly said that ideas are a dime a dozen—often by someone who's never had a good one. If, however, you look at the world's art, invention, scientific discovery, religion, politics and ideology, you will find that what is true for dramatic storytelling is true for all forms of human expression—they are based on quickly communicated, vivid, and memorable ideas.

This is not to suggest that ideas need to be dumbed down. Rather, it is to recognize that the ability to express concepts quickly, simply, and vividly has always been one of the core principles of effective communication. It is not always possible to convey the essence of a story simply, succinctly, and vividly, but it's much more possible than many people think. The inability to do so often stems from not having thought enough about what's really important in a story.

What have sometimes been called "high concepts" are often good examples of what we mean by "story ideas." That is, the idea is not some vague statement like "all men should be brothers" or "life's a bitch," but is instead a concrete juxtaposition of elements that yield an enticing, often unique plot or character element. "Arnold Schwarzenegger and Danny DeVito are twins," the one-line pitch that reputedly led to the very successful film *Twins* (1988), is a classic example. A more recent example is Spike Lee's *Blackkklansman* (2018)—"Black man infiltrates Ku Klux Klan."[6]

It's often a story idea that an aggrieved writer claims to have invented, and they are outraged when others use the same idea. Yet upon closer examination and analysis, it is usually evident that one can list half a dozen famous films that contain the same elements the aggrieved writer is claiming to have uniquely invented.

Writers may believe that they've created something entirely new because they have consumed preexisting material or works but forgotten the source. Or they may not even be aware that what they thought of has already been thought of by someone else. In practice, the effect is the same.

But copyright is not granted because you created something new. It's granted because the something was created *by you.* For more on this, see appendix A, "Copyright Fundamentals."

Free Ideas (Copyright) versus Idea Theft (Contract)

There is federal copyright law, the law of literary and intellectual property. But there is also state contract law, the law of consensual agreements. Although ideas are not treated as protected intellectual property under federal copyright law, in certain situations, they may be protected under state contract law.

In certain contexts—typically a formal pitch meeting in production offices—parties can be found to have entered into an agreement with each other to protect any ideas that are disclosed and pay for any ideas that are used. This applies *even if nothing has been written down.* That is, the agreement need not be in writing, or even expressed.

The agreement could be voiced, but typically it is unspoken and implied by the business context. It is understood that you are there to try to sell, and that the other party is there to (maybe) buy. If you are pitching to a producer or executive, it is this industry practice and understanding that establishes an implied contract.

But the protectable right in these situations does not spring from the idea itself. The idea is unprotected unless and until a protectable right is created by a contract, whether express or implied.

Free as the air.

For more about idea theft, see chapter 4, "Selling to Others."

Idea versus Expression

There is a crucial difference between an idea and the *expression* of an idea.

The problem, though, is that any written text (synopsis, treatment, or script) could be a varying mix of unprotected ideas and protectable expression.[7] As we've seen, ideas are not protected under copyright law. So the general subject matter of your synopsis, treatment, or spec script is an unprotectable idea, even though it has been expressed in writing.

Expression is what copyright law protects. Certainly the verbatim copying of your synopsis, treatment, or script without your permission would be a prohibited infringement under copyright law. But the threshold for infringement is much lower than that for verbatim copying or, as some courts call it, "literal appropriation."[8]

The courts recognize that there is a continuum from specific verbatim expression (protected) to general subject matter or idea (unprotected).[9] But there is no bright-line test. Each case is different and must be examined on its own merits: "If there is substantial similarity in ideas, then [a judge or jury] must decide whether there is substantial similarity in the expressions of the ideas so as to constitute infringement."[10] This analysis is also known as the Abstraction Test.[11] Quite ironic, since the test itself is somewhat abstract in its articulation and application. The concept is that the specific is more protectable than the general.

This is consistent with another concept in copyright law, namely *Scènes à faire*.

SCÈNES À FAIRE

Scènes à faire is a structural concept. A French phrase used in discussing principles of drama, it literally translates to "scenes which must be done."[12] (A gun placed in a drawer in act 1 had better lead to a shooting in act 3.)

Scènes à faire is material that appears often enough in a particular type of work or genre that the material is truly commonplace. Such material can include plot, character, sequence, and setting—many of the same categories that an expert looks at when analyzing substantial similarity. (More on this in chapter 5, "Copyright Infringement.")

A western with a reluctant hero, a gang of villains, a ticking clock, a bar fight, a chase, an ambush, an escape, and a one-on-one final showdown is not copyright infringement. It is simply following the conventions of the genre, and you cannot copyright a convention. A film noir set in the big city, with an underlying crime, a femme fatale, an innocent woman, and a conflicted male lead with a past that has come back to haunt him and who manages to stay one step ahead of law enforcement but one step behind the villains is not copyright infringement. It is simply following the conventions of the genre. No one can own them.

You Probably Didn't Make Up Your Story

If your story is not based upon news, history, biography, facts, or a published work with an expired copyright, then where did it come from? Although some writers will say "I made it all up," such a statement is likely to reveal naivete and a lack of knowledge of the history of their art form.

Western drama has been around for 2,500 years, and if Aristotle, whose study of tragedy is still used in basic dramatic writing courses, were to see films opening in our local multiplexes this week, he would recognize the continuities with the plays he talked about. Over 75,000 feature films have been released in the United States, the vast majority of them adhering to Aristotelian principles. Whether a film's creators intend it or even realize it, their creations are to a large extent the fruit of a tree that was planted at least two thousand years earlier. The modern writer is standing on the shoulders of literary conventions, *scènes à faire*, genre, and genre expectations.

You Probably Didn't Steal Your Story

A trend in the film industry has been to rely on past or "presold" properties created some time ago (e.g., comic books, old films, hit television shows) to produce reboots, sequels, or prequels. This is not something the film and television industries invented. When Sophocles, Aeschylus, and Euripides, some 2,500 years ago, composed dramas for the ancient Greek equivalent of the Academy Awards, they often retold stories the audience was already familiar with. Shakespeare, Marlowe, and the other Elizabethans did the same.

While technology often creates something never before seen in human history, artists *begin* with something known (the stock elements) and then create something new that they graft onto those preexisting elements, adding enough new material to make the work their own.

This is where branding comes in. Manufacturers spend millions, even billions (as Exxon did when it changed its name) branding themselves. AMC spent millions rebranding itself from American Movie Classics, a favorite of old people, into a more hip channel for younger audiences that emphasized original programming. Branding is absolutely crucial. Why? Because that's how people remember you.

Keep this in mind in developing your own personal brand (actors and some writers call this their "voice"). If you are not vivid in some way, how will you be memorable? If your work is not memorable, why should anyone pay any attention to it? And how will they be able to repeat the central idea of your story to others, as development executives must do to their bosses, or as friends do when talking about a film with others?

Even if you wanted to, you personally probably couldn't afford to license or buy the rights to a successful video game, comic book, play, book, or movie. Don't, however say you can't afford branding and give up. There are many ways to brand.

The Sopranos was HBO's biggest success, causing millions of people to subscribe to cable systems or providers that carried HBO. Would *The Sopranos* have been so popular if *The Godfather* weren't still a brand people remembered?

Did the producers of *The Sopranos* pay Paramount for the right to evoke *The Godfather*? Not that we're aware of. *The Sopranos* is a good example of a work coming into existence that's predicated on the existence of a previous work yet avoids infringement. Aside from the font used in the titles, there's nothing in *The Sopranos* that closely imitates (i.e., infringes upon) *The Godfather*.

The world contains an unbelievably rich treasure trove of stories that are yours for the taking. The world is also full of characters you are free to use, as long as they don't come directly from somebody's copyrighted work or aren't identifiable as a specific person. You can use *unprotected* elements and make the work as a whole your own.

In the 1990s, industry wisdom said that docudramas and biopics were box office poison. That's another example of the herd mentality that drives the industry, and that somebody in three or four years will prove wrong. We are not just talking about stories that declare they are based on a real historic figure. We are talking about works that evoke an identifiable persona, whether an actual person, living or dead, or a character from other works of fiction. Evoking is not infringing.

If you're willing to accept the fact that you stand on the shoulders of people who stood on the shoulders of other people, and so on, from time immemorial, then what's wrong with using characters and story elements that don't infringe on somebody else's rights and that will help you find an audience?

Remember the famous quote from Pablo Picasso, "Bad artists copy; great artists steal." We're not suggesting that you violate copyright laws. We urge you use "stealing" the way Picasso intended it, which is to take preexisting elements and make them your own--in other words, use them to create your own brand.

FAIR USE OF COPYRIGHTED WORKS

Even if material is protected under copyright, the Copyright Act expressly grants statutory permission to the public to use copyrighted material for certain uses known as fair use:

> [T]he *fair use of a copyrighted work*, including such use by reproduction in copies or phonorecords or by any other means specified by that section, for purposes such as criticism, comment, news reporting, teaching (including multiple copies for classroom use), scholarship, or research, *is not an infringement of copyright.* [emphasis added][13]

As a user, you do not have to compensate the copyright holder for fair use. Correspondingly, as a copyright holder, you are not compensated for fair use of your copyrighted work by others.

In effect, if the use falls under a statutorily designated use, then it is as though the material were in the public domain and free for the taking. The free statutory uses are referred to as fair use.

Note that the statute lists some permissible purposes, but by its very terms and preamble (i.e., "including such use"), the list is merely suggestive, rather than exclusive or exhaustive. Nowhere, for example, does the statute expressly refer to documentary films. And yet, if you are a documentary filmmaker, you are probably freer to invoke fair use than a dramatic filmmaker would be, because you are more overtly engaging in "criticism, comment, news reporting, [or] teaching."

In determining whether the use made of a work in any particular case is a fair use, the Copyright Act provides a non-exhaustive list of factors to be considered:

1. the purpose and character of the use, including whether such use is of a commercial nature or is for nonprofit educational purposes;
2. the nature of the copyrighted work;
3. the amount and substantiality of the portion used in relation to the copyrighted work as a whole; and
4. the effect of the use upon the potential market for or value of the copyrighted work.[14]

In recent years, fair use issues have been heavily and prominently litigated. Indeed, analysis and discussion of the fair use doctrine could easily be a separate book.

It is important to know that fair use rights exist, and that you do not need permission for everything you take from a copyrighted work. But we suggest that while it is important to understand copyright laws in general, whether your given use of material is fair use *is not something you need to determine yourself.* That will be determined by the companies that distribute the material, using attorneys who are specialists in this area of the law.

CHAPTER TWO

Clearance Required

What You Do Need
Permission to Use

What is clearance? Clearance is an entertainment business term of art. Clearance refers to the analysis and activities necessary to ensure that a project does not infringe on anyone else's rights (i.e., third-party rights). That means the copyrights of other authors as well as the personal rights of any living person or deceased celebrity.

A work is deemed clear of infringements, which means any third-party material used in the work is public domain material,[1] or protected material used with the express written permission of the rights holder. A work is cleared as non-infringing by the studio attorneys and insurers before public distribution and exhibition.

CLEARANCE FROM THE WRITER'S POINT OF VIEW

As a writer, you should be aware of clearance issues, but don't obsess over them. Leave that to the producers and distributors, and their lawyers and insurers. When clearance is in doubt, it is their role to mitigate risk, not yours as a writer.

The mindset we encourage for writers is that you should not self-censor with clearance issues before coming up with your stories. Come up with your stories first. Then do a clearance analysis after.

This chapter is about what red flags should pop up in a clearance analysis and, most importantly, what you should do about those clearance issues.

PREEXISTING MATERIAL

On the one hand, consider everything you read, hear, or see—whether in books, newspapers, on the internet, or any other place—to be copyrighted. On the other hand, much of what is claimed to be copyrighted is not actually protectable by copyright law.

Ideas and facts, remember, are free for the taking. The execution itself (i.e., expression) is protected, but that's it. The idea underlying the expression is as free for you to take as it was for the creator who used it before you.

What does that mean for you as a writer in practical terms?

No genre film can legally prevent other films from being made in that genre. Based upon the conventions—indeed, requirements—of any given genre, there will be similarities in the structure and narrative of films within that genre. Similarities are inevitable. That's just *scènes à faire*.[2] Narrative structure and its necessary causality are not protected by copyright.

For example, at some level, all plague films look the same: An epidemic has broken out, and our disenfranchised loner hero, while fending off those already infected, races against time to find the cause—and then the cure—to save the world and find redemption. And using a plague as a dramatic catalyst for an action adventure saga is certainly not novel or new. Take a look at *The Iliad* or the Book of Exodus. *Contagion* (2011) was not stopped by *Outbreak* (1995), which was not stopped by *The Andromeda Strain* (1971). *I am Legend* (2007) was not stopped by 28 *Days Later* (2002), which was not stopped by 12 *Monkeys* (1995). We could go on, but you get the idea. Dozens of plague films have been made over the past fifty years or so. Their creators were not copyright infringers. They were smart storytellers adhering to the tried-and-true conventions of the plague film genre.

Do You Need Their Story to Tell Your Story?

Let's say you fall in love with a very successful series of children's novels about a girl who acquires a magical flashlight. When she shines it on objects or people, she sees into their real essence, and can even enter into other realms and physical spaces merely by pointing her flashlight at them, but what she keeps discovering at the end of each book in the series is that her real power lies within.

If you go to the writer or agent of this very successful series and ask for permission to make your film, you will, if you do not have access to a large sum of money, likely be laughed at. And you will have closed the door on yourself, because you will have (implicitly) acknowledged that you were knowingly basing your work on that of the author.

This is one of the risks of asking permission—in an overabundance of caution—when you don't really need it.

By asking for permission, you act as though you actually—artistically and legally—need it. At least in the novelist's mind or the life-story subject's mind, asking for permission implicitly acknowledges your reliance on their material. And this implicitly concedes that the material that you used is protected, even if it is unprotected fact or purely unprotectable *scènes à faire*.

Perhaps there is a more strategic approach to the material.

How many stories have there been about a young person who acquires a powerful amulet or object that has magical or supernatural powers? King Arthur had Excalibur and Dorothy, in *The Wizard of Oz*, had her red shoes. What happens to Excalibur? In some of the most popular versions, it ends up at the bottom of the lake. In *The Wizard of Oz*, Glinda tells Dorothy that the power she's been seeking throughout the film is one she's always had. Memorable popular films are full of stories of young people who acquire what they think is a powerful external object, only to realize that the power lies within themselves.

Does your source have a source? Often, the idea, situation, plot, or character that you so want to use was used earlier by some writer who came *before* the writer you think "owns" it. If so, you are as entitled as they were to use basic story ideas, plots, themes, and so on. You'd both be borrowing—not stealing—from the same source.

Once again, it's important to remember that ideas are not copyrightable—only the expression is. Much of the time, it's possible to use similar story elements, as long as you express them in your own way. But make the story truly yours, not just an imitation of someone else's.

Acquiring a Short Story

Let's suppose that you really do need the rights to some else's short story to make your film. That is, you're not using just the idea, or general themes and situations, or stock characters. You actually want to use specific characters, scenes, and dialogue for a faithful adaptation. How can you—a person with no power, no significant money, no industry credibility—acquire the rights to someone's short story, novel, or other fictional work?

As demonstrated by *Brokeback Mountain, The Shawshank Redemption,* and *Stand by Me,* to name just a few memorable films, short stories are often a great source of film stories. Some years ago, Francis Ford Coppola said in Howard's class at UCLA that he thought short stories were a great untapped wellspring for film. About a year later, Coppola started publishing the magazine *All-Story* (www.all-story.com), which is devoted to short works of fiction. Not long after, he made the critically acclaimed *Youth without Youth,* based on a novella by the Romanian mythologist and author Mircea Eliade.

From an artistic standpoint, one reason short stories are good sources of material is because, like most memorable popular films, they are generally structured around a single character and a single central problem that must be resolved. Thus, the structure comes ready-made, unlike most novels, which almost invariably require many rewrites and much restructuring before a film's creators can figure out what it's about (and often, who). When you adapt a short story, there is still plenty of room to make it your own. You are free to add subplots and additional situations and characters. Adapting a short story is often an additive process—unlike adapting a novel, which, at least in the first pass, is largely a pruning or subtractive process. There's also an economic aspect to basing a film on a short story. There's little market for short stories and therefore little potential revenue. Thus, they are easier to acquire and can be had for less money than most novels. Novelists— and their agents and publishers—dream of the (largely mythical) Big Hollywood Sale. In the first few years after a novel's publication, it's probably useless for you to try to acquire the rights to the book, because the author is still dreaming that Steven Spielberg will call.

But when a short story is involved, everybody—even and especially the author—knows there's little likelihood of significant upfront money arriving on their doorstep. Even though you may be an impoverished filmmaker, you offer the short story writer the potential of having a film based on their work that might not otherwise exist.

Acquiring a Novel

If you're a film student or a first-time filmmaker, it is likely easier and cheaper (and perhaps even less time consuming) for you to write a novel yourself than it is for you to get the rights to someone else's published novel.

If you are insistent on adapting a novel, it would probably be advisable to think in terms of old novels that were published, say, fifty or more years ago. The older the better. If the novel is old enough, the copyright may well have expired and the book will have fallen into the public domain (e.g., anything by Jane Austen, Charles Dickens, Mary Shelley, Herman Melville, H. G. Wells, Arthur Conan Doyle).

But be cautious, and be objective. If the novel's been lying around a long time and no one in the film industry has optioned or bought it, there may be a good reason for that. Perhaps nobody's thought of a way they could adapt the novel into a watchable film or series. But don't stop with that thought. Instead, consider whether you have a solution to the problems that may have stumped others. If you have a viable solution, maybe it's worth investing the time (your most precious commodity) in it.

An Alternate Way to Acquire Rights

If you are a new writer, director, or producer, you may rule out the idea of acquiring a novel, short story, or other existing intellectual property because you have no reputation and, equally important, no money to pay others. It would be naive to go after best-selling or famous works, but the world is full of story material that you might be able to get the rights to for little or no advance payment.

As a beginning creator, you probably can't compete with Hollywood studios or networks. But there are many wonderful stories that the studios or networks have not tried to buy. In such cases, your lack of money may not totally prevent you from acquiring the work.

It is important to distinguish between buying a work outright and buying an option that gives you the exclusive right to buy the work within a certain time period. Options are always less expensive than outright purchases, and perhaps easier for you to get.

Someone who options something has the right, for a stipulated period of time, to advance the work's potential to be produced. In other words, you walk the project around town looking for production money. But you need the option rights in hand to be able to do so. Because if you get a producer interested in the story but you don't have the rights locked with an option, the producer could just go around you and get the rights directly, and then you're permanently out of the picture.

There are some sensitive, intelligent, fearful writers out there who are afraid that if they sign over the rights to their baby, those Hollywood pimps will put it out on the street to turn tricks for foreign tourists. Therefore, if you are young and relatively inexperienced, it is *possible* that the author of an original work might trust you if you come across as being really committed to their work and provide evidence that you know what needs to be done to bring the story to the screen in a thoughtful and sensitive way, respecting the underlying source material.

Since we assume you will not have enough money to buy the property, you will probably want to option it. Options are commonly obtained for a few thousand dollars, and sometimes as little as one dollar. But the chances are good that what you can afford to offer as option money is not going to be sufficiently lucrative to change any author's life. So, consider what else you can offer an author aside from money.

If you say to someone, "I'd like to become your partner in turning this story into a film, and I'm willing to share X percent of anything I get paid as a writer with you," this can be a meaningful offer. But you need to make your offer to the right person. It is probably best to make such an offer directly to the author, not to their manager and definitely not to their agent. They get paid a percentage of what the author receives, and if no money is changing hands at the beginning, they may have no interest in taking a chance on you.

What percentage should you offer? That's up to you. Offering to go fifty-fifty is more likely to be persuasive than any other percentage, because it underlines the idea of partnership. Some people might think it's too generous. But remember that you may have other income streams from the project. For example, perhaps you will also want to be one of the producers, or maybe the director—and for that you would receive a separate fee that you have no need to share.

In the mirror image of the discussion above, let's turn to another issue.

What Do You Need Them For?

Let's go back to what should be your first question when you think of asking someone for the rights to their work. What do you need them for?

This question applies not only to novels and short stories, but also to newspaper or magazine articles, biographies, stage plays, and any other source of material you find. Are you really planning to use *protected* material?

In our experience, all too many creative people think they need to pay somebody if they consciously use anything from another work. But such a belief may confuse plagiarism with copyright infringement. When you were young, you were taught to always give credit to the author of something you took from another source. But this is an academic rule, not the law of copyright. See appendix A, "Copyright Fundamentals."

All creators stand on the shoulders of creators who preceded them. Very often, writers, consciously or unconsciously, develop stories whose conception can be traced from other stories they've encountered sometime in their lives. A famous book by the nineteenth-century French writer Georges Polti asserted that there were thirty-six basic plots. Others have put the number lower, a few higher, but seldom has anyone gone over fifty. So when you write a story, the chances are good you did not invent the plot totally on your own. Chances are good that major elements of it have been used before and will be used by many others in the future. You may feel your story is new, but it probably is only new to you.

We're trying to liberate you from the misconceptions that lead you to think you need permission to use anything that didn't begin in your own mind. We are not urging you to steal, but helping you understand what you are legally free to use.

Franchise Specs (aka Writing Samples)

From time to time, it has been in vogue for beginning writers to pen a writing sample spec based upon franchise material from a preexisting series. For a while there, everyone had a *Simpsons* or *South Park* spec in the closet. But who owns that spec?

We thought you'd find this (true) story interesting:

An actor wrote and starred in a series of commercially successful films. A screenwriter, after viewing the third movie in the series, wrote a spec treatment for a fourth movie. The spec incorporated the characters created by the actor in his prior films in the franchise, and even cited the actor as a coauthor. The screenwriter then met with studio executives to discuss the treatment.

The studio passed. The studio later released a fourth movie with some similarity to the treatment. The writer of the spec script filed suit, alleging idea theft.

The result? The court held, among other things, that the treatment was not entitled to copyright protection because the screenwriter appropriated characters developed by the actor and created a derivative work without permission. That means the spec screenwriter was the copyright infringer, even though the screenwriter had penned a new sequel for the franchise.

This is the true story of a spec for *Rocky IV*.[3]

Bottom line: If your spec is unauthorized—even if it's just a calling-card writing sample written in the hopeful good faith of getting a writing assignment—it is technically a copyright infringement and is essentially free for use by the true copyright holder/author. Do not write specs based upon someone else's preexisting and protected work. Your spec will not be yours to sell.

LIFE RIGHTS: USING THE LIVES OF OTHERS

Biographical pictures, or biopics, dramatize the lives of actual persons. Biopics have been popular almost as long as motion pictures have been popular. But no one's life fits neatly into an entertaining narrative structure. Inevitably, a biopic screenwriter must pick and choose events to include or exclude. Sometimes, biopics stretch the truth and dramatize a life story with varying degrees of accuracy.

So, if you want to make a biopic about someone, should you get their permission? *Must* you get their permission?

First Amendment, First and Foremost

There is a widely held misconception in the entertainment industry that a screenwriter or filmmaker is legally required to obtain the consent—a life rights agreement—from persons (if living) or their estates (if deceased) before using them as the subject of a film. And that if you don't, the person or estate could legally block the film and recover monetary damages. Not true.

The law does not require life rights agreements.[4] Indeed, the term "life rights" is somewhat of a misnomer, because no one owns the facts that make up the narrative of their life. As you will recall, facts are free for the taking.

But what if you know the biopic facts only through published source material? Do you need to get clearance to use the source material?

The film *There Will Be Blood* (2007) won two Academy Awards, including Best Performance by an Actor in a Leading Role (Daniel Day-Lewis). In an Associated Press interview, director Paul Thomas Anderson revealed he drew much of his inspiration for the acclaimed film from the biography of oil tycoon Edward Doheny, *Dark Side of Fortune*, written by Margaret Leslie Davis and published by the University of California Press in 1998. Inspiration is not infringement. Inspiration is free for the taking.

An inexperienced filmmaker probably would have wasted valuable time and financial resources trying to lock up the rights to the book. But the more experienced filmmaker knows when to use a preexisting work as a jumping-off point for their own. The moral of the story is, of course, don't pay for that which you can use for free (or at least let the studio worry about doing that for you). Facts about history and historical persons are free for the taking.

The widely held misconception that screenwriters and filmmakers need to obtain life rights for biopics is probably a result of entertainment industry widespread custom and practice and/or an overly expansive reading of the rights of publicity. Both are discussed in the following sections.

Custom and Practice: Advantages to Getting Life Rights

Film investors, financiers, distributors, and insurers are concerned about financial risk, and focus on ways to minimize risk. Obtaining consent in a life rights agreement from the subject person(s) certainly helps reduce the risk of litigation (frivolous or otherwise) and interference with production or distribution. Life rights agreements have become part of the required clearance package for biopics. But that's something that the producer is concerned with as part of packaging the project. That's not something that writers necessarily need to worry about.

Nevertheless, are there artistic reasons for a writer to try to get the subject's life rights? Yes, especially in the early stages of writing. Cooperation can be priceless. The person (if alive) or estate representative (if the subject is deceased) may grant you access to very useful and otherwise private materials, including notes, diaries, and photos, as well as share unpublished anecdotes. Not only can having such access help make your project stronger, but also it can give you a competitive advantage over any others pursuing the same biopic without authorization or cooperation.

Rights of Publicity and Commercial Misappropriation

The right of publicity protects against the unauthorized use of a person's name, voice, signature, photograph, or likeness for products, merchandising, or advertising. In California, the right of publicity exists for all living persons[5] and any deceased celebrities.[6] Violation of the right to publicity is referred to as commercial misappropriation.

Even though we may think of film as a product in the stream of commerce, film is first and foremost one of the "useful arts."[7] Films, plays, television programs, books, and articles are "expressive works" protected by the First

Amendment and are not considered products or merchandise for purposes of rights of publicity and commercial misappropriation.[8] The merchandise or products that give rise to a commercial misappropriation claim are items such as t-shirts and lithographs,[9] greeting cards,[10] and video games,[11] as well as merchandise or product advertisements and endorsements.[12]

Indeed, the California commercial misappropriation statute for deceased celebrities expressly excludes "fictional or nonfictional entertainment."[13] So biopics are fair—and free—game.

CHAPTER THREE

Collaboration

A spec writer, working alone, has all the power over their project. The power of ownership. The power of control. But when working in collaboration with others, this power dynamic changes. Collaboration necessarily raises issues of *shared* ownership and control.

Typically, collaboration questions come up in two general situations:

1. Concerns about the downside. A writer wants to collaborate, but doesn't know what steps to take to collaborate "safely." In this situation, "safely," usually refers to legal safety, but artistic and creative safety are just as important.

2. Questions about the upside. A writer is trying to decide whether collaborating is beneficial to their overall career: Do I stand a better chance if I team up with someone? If so, what are the characteristics of the person I should team up with?

No one can decide for you whether you should collaborate. Our goal is to better inform your decision. To that end, this chapter explores the artistic and business advantages and disadvantages of collaboration.

A COLLABORATIVE BUSINESS?

What is collaboration? In the broadest sense, collaboration is defined as working together and/or working on a common goal. The cliché that film and television are collaborative businesses is absolutely true. Yet most writers write alone.

Collaboration has become a buzzword devoid of meaning for most persons buzzing it. Cooperation is not necessarily collaboration. For example, consecutive work on different parts of a project by different persons does not constitute collaboration. That's an assembly line model with a division of labor.

The type of teamwork between or among writers that results in coauthorship is something else. The writers are working—planning, plotting, arguing, deciding—together (even if they're writing separately) on the same script.

In collaboration—as in life—you should not expect pure equality. Someone will always give more effort. Someone will always create more pages. Someone is always better. But you don't want to feel taken advantage of by your writing partner. In entering into a collaboration relationship, aligning your expectations and those of your collaborator(s) is the key.

SHOULD YOU COLLABORATE?

Your heart may want to collaborate without your head knowing why. It just feels right, you say. Fair enough. Far be it for us to act as the protective parents who try to dissuade you from eloping. Go for it!

But if your head is second-guessing your heart, we can offer an analytical framework to examine the ways in which collaboration might be advantageous.

First, let's be reminded of the default position: *When in doubt, write alone.*

You should collaborate *only if* your collaborator will contribute something of value that is necessary for the project. That means actual writing or rewriting, not merely brainstorming ideas or giving script notes.

Writing can be a lonely activity. Too often writers collaborate to have the company of a cowriter.

But companionship is not enough of a reason to collaborate. Sure, you are not alone anymore, but you might not be advancing your project either. And if the relationship doesn't advance the project, then you'll be lonely together.

What contributions advance a project? First and foremost, each cowriter must write. Otherwise a writers' collaboration agreement is not appropriate, because you're not collaborating writers.

If not everyone is writing, you still may be working collaboratively, but just not as coauthors. Perhaps your team consists of a writer and a producer? If so, an attachment agreement is more appropriate. We discuss that a bit later in this chapter.

Only the actual writer(s) should be the author(s) and therefore be entitled to copyright protection.

COLLABORATION ESSENTIALS

The number of people who collaborate on making an independent film can be as low as a few dozen, although between a hundred and two hundred people is closer to the norm. Blockbuster films can require a thousand to three thousand people to reach the screen. It is no wonder, then, that the ability to collaborate is one of the most important skills for anyone working in film.

Writers of screenplays may think of themselves as poets or artists, at least while they work alone, yet most films are written by several people. For the film or television writer, collaboration can be a choice or a necessity. For those who choose to collaborate in the writing phase, there are many things to consider.

In many collaborations of writers, the people involved first come together not to produce a work, but as friends who respect and admire each other. After this has happened, the urge often strikes both to say, "Let's do something together." The friendship that preceded the collaboration is often as valuable to the collaborators as the specific project. As with any interpersonal relationship, as time goes on, things change, frictions can develop, and the personal relationship, or what once was the personal relationship, can become problematic and even difficult to handle.

Friendship is not necessary for collaboration. The members of an orchestra gather together for a specific performance, and while there may be other performances, the quality of the music they produce is not necessarily helped or hindered by the quality of their interpersonal relationships.

In film, especially in writing, it often becomes difficult to separate the personal relationship from the project. The decision to collaborate is usually based on some vague idea of mutuality of effort and a fifty-fifty split of any money, credit, awards, and so on. But it is entirely all too human that one party or the other begins to feel that he or she has contributed more work—or better work—and therefore deserves a greater share of the proceeds. When conflicts arise, one or both collaborators may declare, "If you were really my friend . . . " And both may feel hurt and betrayed.

It is useful to think of how collaboration is similar to, but also different from, a love relationship. Both begin with feelings of affinity and require people to spend a lot of time with one other. In love, however, the relationship is its own justification and reason for being—there is no goal other than to continue the relationship.

In a partnership, there clearly *is* a goal, and the goal is the justification for the relationship. It is common for people creating a film to say that they did something "for the good of the picture," expressing the primacy of the end product over the relationship that produced it. There are of course marriages where the couple remain together "for the good of the children," which may be considered analogous, but the children are not a "product" similar to a screenplay or finished film.

Should you collaborate? We commonly speak of "falling in love," as though it's beyond our will (or at least our conscious will). But nobody "falls" into collaboration, or should. Collaborators would be well served to compile an objective listing of the gains and liabilities that are likely from a collaboration. Some of the issues you might consider follow.

What Do You Need the Other Person For?

Some people are good at creating interesting plots but have trouble with characterization. Others create engaging dialogue but have trouble with structure. It is seldom that a single writer is equally good at plot, structure, dialogue, characterization, and creating memorable scenes. If collaborators have complementary strengths, they may need each other.

What Do They Need You For?

You may be clear about what you need. What about your collaborator(s)? Do they feel that *you* bring complementary strengths to the table?

Will You Work Faster or Slower with a Collaborator?

Speed, at least in film, is not always important, and it may be that while collaborating will slow you down in some ways, it will get you to your final goal faster. Having a collaborator helps avoid writer's block, procrastination, and losing steam. The obligation to pull your share of the project often helps people be productive.

Sometimes people collaborate because they can complete projects faster than they could alone. This is true when both are equally matched in writing strength and divide the workload so they work simultaneously but on different parts of the project. This is especially useful for the fast-paced system of production used in television; it might not be that important in the much more slowly paced world of film production.

Will Each of You Bring Different Perspectives?

Different perspectives can be really valuable because the process of resolving differences can lead to the creation of something neither party could produce alone. But it can also produce creative differences that drive collaborators apart.

Will You Get Along?

This is like any close relationship—it is not possible to know until you've tried it. People fall in love for any number of reasons, but they frequently fall *out* of love because they've fallen out of respect. You cease to admire their work, their commitment, their ideas of what the story is about, their humor, and sometimes even their personal habits. Whatever the reasons, if you lose respect for your collaborator, it's hard to maintain a close relationship.

Will You Continue to Like Them?

This is not the same question as "Will you get along?" To work together, there must be mutual respect on some level and you will need to get along. But you don't have to like your collaborator. Your primary job is to *work* together, not like each other.

If liking were a requirement, few films would ever begin and even fewer would be completed. When writers seek our advice about failing or failed collaborations, we usually ask them what led them to collaborate together in the first place. The answer is almost always "We liked each other." It's comfortable to work with people you like, but it is not necessary. For amateurs, the relationship drives the project. But for professionals, the project drives the relationship.

What's the Cost of Collaboration?

We're not referring primarily to the amount of money you hope to make. Obviously, collaborators have to share some of the money they might have kept for themselves if they worked alone.

More important, we think, is what collaboration costs you in terms of your own creativity. Collaboration should have the result that the two of you working together are *more* creative than if you'd worked separately. If maintaining the collaborative arrangement begins to take excessive time and energy from your productivity, then perhaps it's time for you both to go your separate ways. This is not easy to determine.

Are You Seeking to Use Your Collaborator's Power?

There is nothing wrong if this is the case. The best collaboration is when you *complement* each other. If your collaborator is good at plotting and you are good at structure, you both become stronger by contributions of different strengths. Your collaborator may have more experience and contacts, which you will match with the brilliance of your dialogue and structure.

The danger, of course, is that the exchange of powers may not be equitable or even reciprocal, which leads to the loss of respect previously discussed.

How Will You Each Handle Conflict?

As in a marriage, conflicts are inevitable. As in a marriage, how each party *handles* conflicts is an important part of resolving them. Conflicts must be handled fairly and efficiently. If all of your energies are spent on maintaining the relationship in the face of conflicts, the result may be that neither of you is being as productive or creative as you would have been with a different collaborator or even by yourself.

COAUTHORSHIP = CO-OWNERSHIP

A successful collaboration results in a coauthored work. The required elements for coauthorship are:

- two or more writers,
- working on the same script, and
- intending their work to result in a single, unified script.[1]

If each of those three elements is present, then you are coauthors.[2] And coauthors means co-owners.[3]

Under copyright law, each and every owner has the legal authority to grant permission to others to distribute, reproduce, or create derivative works based on the copyrighted material.[4]

Yes, you read that correctly—each and every coauthor has independent and full authority to sign away any and all of the copyright rights.

This rule is particularly dangerous for you as a writer if your manager/agent/friend decides that they're coauthor of your work and therefore can shop the work around and sell it out from under you. Stay connected with the business and sales plan.

Also, even if you have a true writers' relationship and a cocktail-napkin agreement that says "everything" is fifty-fifty, either of you can sell the whole. You may be the primary author, but for a buyer (producer) to obtain the rights, they only need one of the cowriters to sign away the rights. Each writer has an undivided ownership in the entire script. For more on this issue, please see appendix B, "Collaboration Problems."

When Should I Use a Written Collaboration Agreement?

Whenever you're not working alone!

We can't tell you how many times screenwriters have come to us complaining that their (former) partner has done them wrong. Almost invariably, the screenwriters who have problems are working together without a collaboration agreement.

If you are in any way working with someone else, all participants should have a clear understanding about the nature of their relationship and ownership and control of any resulting work product.

If you haven't put this in writing, you may very well regret it later. The best way to clarify everyone's understanding is through a written agreement signed by the parties to evidence their understanding.

Does a Collaboration Agreement Need to Be in Writing?

Legally, no. But practically, yes.

Legally, no: The law does not require that a collaboration agreement be in writing. Copyright law does require the transfer of interests in intellectual property to be in writing to be enforceable.[5] But coauthorship is not a transfer of rights; it is the joint creation of authorship rights.

The Copyright Act provides that a transfer of copyright ownership "is not valid unless an instrument of conveyance, or a note or memorandum of the transfer, is in writing and signed by the owner of the rights conveyed or such owner's duly authorized agent."[6] Any claim of ownership based on an oral agreement or the existence of a partnership or joint venture is barred by the Copyright Act.[7]

However, as we've tried to emphasize above, transfer of ownership is not required if the parties are joint authors. Joint authors are already joint owners.[8]

Practically, yes: It's certainly a smart idea to put your deal in writing. By memorializing everyone's understanding and agreement about the nature of the relationship and about the ownership and control of the property, the door is closed to later arguments and assertions that the relationship was something else, or that ownership and control were somehow different. Indeed, the best and most objective "manifestation of shared intent" is a written contract that states that the parties intend—*or do not intend*—to be coauthors.[9]

When Should We Enter into a Collaboration Agreement?

Before you collaborate. The best chance of getting a mutually acceptable collaboration agreement signed is

- *before* any work is done by anyone,
- *before* any disagreements have come up, and certainly
- *before* any money is on the table and a potential buyer is waiting in the wings.

You will note that there is a running concept here—*before*. Because once the collaboration is under way, and work has been done, or disagreements have arisen, or there is a potential buyer, the relative bargaining power in the room will likely change.

The starting point is when everyone has equal bargaining power and everyone is most optimistic about the process and project ahead. And if at the beginning you don't have equal bargaining power or are not optimistic about the adventure ahead, then it begs the question of whether you should be working together in the first place.

What Should Be Included in a Collaboration Agreement?

At the very least, a collaboration agreement should

- identify the project,
- identify the writers,
- state what each writer is required to do (i.e., write/ rewrite), and
- state what each writer will get in return (i.e., percentage share).

What's a fair split? We've always liked fifty-fifty for projects that are starting from scratch. It is an endorsement of equality and parity. But maybe one of you already has a draft, and the second collaborator is being brought in mid-project. Perhaps the first writer should get a bit more? It depends.

Whatever the two (or more) of you agree to, that's what your collaboration agreement should reflect.

Intent is key. What you intend needs to be in sync with what everyone else intends.

What If We're Already Collaborating but Haven't Signed an Agreement?

You still might have an enforceable collaboration agreement—just not a written one.

Did you discuss the nature of your working together? Did you have a "handshake" agreement but never put it in writing? Have you been writing together for some time now? Have you been working together in a way that's consistent with your handshake agreement?

The absence of a written and signed agreement doesn't mean that there's no agreement. It just means there's no *written* agreement. You may well have an oral agreement or an implied-in-fact agreement.

But the lack of written agreement does make determining the precise terms of the agreement more complicated. What, in fact, is the actual and specific nature of the relationship? What was the expected contribution from the participants?

It's best to discuss these issues and put your mutual understanding in writing at the beginning of the project. That's when both parties have equal bargaining power, and you can most effectively set and clarify roles and responsibilities. Earlier is better than later, but it's never too late to sign a collaboration agreement.

Do We Need to Address Credits in the Collaboration Agreement?

Yes, you should. But doing so will not necessarily be the final determination.

The collaboration agreement is binding between you and your collaborator(s). And that is important, as it may determine writing credits. Presumably, you have agreed to share writing credits equally as cowriters. Otherwise, why are you collaborating?

But if your script comes under the jurisdiction of the WGA West, then ultimately the Writers Guild of America determines final credits under the guild rules.[10] The guild would have jurisdiction if you're a guild member, or if a guild signatory, such as the production company that buys your spec, becomes involved in the project.

When screen credits are being determined, those who have participated are given a chance to claim what they think is fair credit, and the producer or production company can state how they think the credits should be allotted. But if any of the writers disagree, the guild rules will be the final arbiter of credits.

Partners, producers, production companies, and others may tell a writer that they will be given such-and-such a credit, but any professional in film and television knows that ultimately the person making the promise does not have final authority to grant it.

If I Take Script Notes from Someone, Is that Person Now a Collaborator?

No. (Again, *no!*)

Whether you're taking notes from others as you develop your script (e.g., from idea through first draft in a writers' group), or take notes on a completed draft, the note giver is not a coauthor.

First and foremost, both parties must intend to have a coauthorship relationship.

You certainly don't intend that when you "workshop" your project in a room with other writers who are likewise workshopping their projects. And when you ask a colleague to read your script and give you input, input is exactly your intent, not a cowriter collaboration. Of course, your intention would seem otherwise if you handed a colleague your script with the request to "rewrite this for me." Second, the prevailing view is that each coauthor must contribute independently copyrightable material.[11] Notes and comments on a script seldom, if ever, rise to that level. Notes and comments, no matter how smart and insightful, are merely suggestions for "fixes," not the actual fixes themselves. Fixing means writing.

Collaboration Is Not (Necessarily) Partnership

Writers often refer to their cowriters as their "writing partner."

In lay terms, *partner* connotes a mutuality. Share and share alike. A team. We're in this together. But in legal terms, it begs the question: What exactly is the "it" that you are in together?

Partnership is something more than mere collaboration. Perhaps the most significant difference is the *fiduciary duty of loyalty* that partners owe to each other. If you're truly partners in the legal sense, and owe a fiduciary duty to each other, it necessarily changes how you deal with the industry at large.

For example, if you're in a writing partnership and someone approaches you to write a project, or if you happen to see an advertisement on a Listserv for a writer, your duty to loyalty is to the existing partnership, and that trumps your own self-interest as an individual writer.

You would need to give the partnership first shot at the other opportunity.

You can't compete with the partnership as an individual writer.

And even if the partnership passes on pursuing the writing opportunity, you still may not be able to take it yourself, because that other writing project might interfere with your partnership writing commitments.

One of the many good reasons for having a written collaboration agreement is so you can affirmatively state that you do not intend to be partners or create a partnership. You merely intend to collaborate in writing a specific project.

COLLABORATING WITH NON-WRITERS:
PRODUCER'S ATTACHMENT AGREEMENTS

A common form of collaboration often develops between a spec writer and an unfunded or underfunded producer, often a first-time producer. Although the participants are not cowriters, the result may nevertheless be a spec script. This is a development relationship wherein the writer writes and the producer guides the writing with notes and ideas (but is not actually writing).

As long as the participants are clear on the nature of the relationship and are in agreement about the desired outcome, writer-producer collaborations can be very fruitful.

A spec writer would like to know that there is someone who is at least interested in moving forward with the script when it's completed. For spec writers without an agent (i.e., most spec writers), that next-best someone would be a producer. That is, a producer who loves the spec's concept but still needs to see the execution.

But producers always want to shape scripts to make them as marketable as possible: marketable to investors, marketable to talent, and marketable to an audience. So the producer may brainstorm story ideas at the beginning, and may give notes along the way, *but* the producer is not writing. The writer is off alone, writing solo. Both the writer and the producer add value to the spec project, but a writers' collaboration agreement would not accurately reflect the reality of the relationship.

In this situation, most reputable producers will use an attachment agreement. An attachment agreement gives the producer the exclusivity they need and acknowledges their sweat equity and contributions (e.g., script notes).

But an attachment agreement does not pretend to treat a nonwriter as a writer.

WHEN A COWRITER DOESN'T WRITE

Who is the author and owner of a script when only one member of the collaboration team does substantially all of the writing? The answer turns on two issues: the screenwriter's intent and the copyrightability of each writer's contributions.

The majority rule for coauthorship/co-ownership requires that collaborators

· intended to be coauthors, and
· have each independently made *copyrightable contributions* to the work.[12]

Intent: The collaborators must "entertain in their minds the concept of joint authorship" such that they "fully intend to be joint authors."[13] Did you discuss being coauthors? Did you agree to be coauthors? Do you have a signed collaboration agreement that says you'll be coauthors? Do the drafts of the script have both your names on them? Have you referred to yourselves as coauthors in reaching out to any third parties (e.g., in inquiry letters to managers, agents, actors, directors, producers)? These are the facts that would evidence your intent or lack of intent.

Copyrightability: Each purported joint author must have contributed copyrightable expression to the work. You don't have to write in the same place, or write at the same time, or write equal amounts, or write equally well to be collaborators.[14] But you both must be writing.

Warning: This is the majority rule (in California and New York, most prominently).[15] There is a *minority view* (in Chicago) that mere intent alone is legally sufficient for a finding of coauthorship.

So if you're working in Chicago, or a jurisdiction that follows the minority/Chicago view, you'd better make sure that your collaboration agreement specifies remedies if one writer doesn't write. Nonwriting should be a material breach of the agreement, and the writing screenwriter should be able to terminate the agreement and walk away with their own work product free and clear of the failed collaboration.

For further reading on this problem, of if you simply enjoy watching an all-too-familiar train wreck, please see appendix B., "Collaboration Problems."

CHAPTER FOUR

Selling to Others and Implied-in-Fact Contracts

ACCESS, ACCESS, ACCESS

As you've probably heard, in real estate it's location, location, location. In selling your script, it's access, access, access.

When you've written and rewritten your script and you feel confident it's as good as you can make it, then (and only then) is it time to start selling. We make this point because, far too often, beginning screenwriters send their work out saying, "I know it needs work, but I'd like to get your reaction." This is unbelievably insulting to the busy and successful people you're trying to impress. If you know it "needs work," why are you wasting their time by sending it out now?

Two variables determine whether your spec will sell. One variable you can control (quality), the other you cannot control (the market).

How do you control quality? There are hundreds of screenwriting books to instruct you about learning the

craft and knowing your projects, not to mention the grow-
ing cottage industry of script consultants. Bottom line,
there's lots of advice out there on how to improve the quality of your spec.

But even with the many screenwriting resources in
print, there is a psychological and motivational issue that's
seldom squarely addressed: the concept of exorcism versus
payday.

Your best projects force you to write them. You cannot
help but write them. They haunt you until you've written
them. You have to get them out.

And so you do, often in a blur of frantically wonderful
compressed time. You're writing from your heart, you're
writing from your soul. And you're trying to exorcise the
story from your soul.

And then you do. It's out, it's done. You've tapped into
the energy of an exorcism. But how far can that exorcism
energy take you after you've written the demons out? Maybe
a rewrite, or two or three? Maybe more. Maybe not. At
some point, the demons are so exorcised that your emotional need to get this story out of your soul has passed.
You've given birth. Let someone else raise this kid? No, but
it's time to move from your heart to your head and use the
analytical tools from all those screenwriting guides.

You must be ready to sell, to go to market. Because
there's no pulling a project back to try again. Once it's out
there, it's out there. There are only a limited number of
buyers to show it to. And they'll only look at it once.

Let's assume that you have genuinely given it your all
and feel the script is ready. As the novelist Salman Rushdie

has advised, "There's a point at which you're not making it better; you're just making it different. You have to be good at recognizing that point."[1]

Selling, first and foremost, requires access. You need access to potential buyers. Who are the buyers? Do you already have access to them? If not, how to you get it? And at what risk?

AIR THAT'S NOT SO FREE: *DESNY V. WILDER*

Generally speaking, ideas are "free as the air," as copyright law does not protect ideas. There are, however, certain circumstances in which ideas can be protected under *contract* law.

There are two ways that a writer brings ideas to a producer or production company:

· by submitting a writing reflecting the idea, that is, an inquiry letter, synopsis, treatment, or spec script, and/or

· through an oral pitch.

Few production companies today will accept unsolicited scripts, largely because of a famous lawsuit that occurred many decades ago. If there's one story from the case law books that every writer should know, it's *Desny v. Wilder.*[2]

In 1949, Victor Desny, an aspiring screenwriter, telephoned the office of the powerful and famous writer/director Billy Wilder at Paramount. Desny asked to see Mr. Wilder, but after some back and forth, Desny pitched

Wilder's secretary a story based on the real life of Floyd
Collins, a cave explorer who was trapped in a cave-in that
grabbed national attention for weeks in 1925. Desny said
that Wilder and Paramount

> could use the story only if they paid him "the reasonable
> value of it. . . . I made it clear to her that I wrote the story and
> that I wanted to sell it. . . . [Wilder's secretary] said that if
> Billy Wilder of Paramount uses the story 'naturally we will
> pay you for it.'"[3]

In a subsequent phone conversation with the secretary,
Desny was told that Paramount had no interest in his
work. But then in 1951, Paramount released *Ace in the
Hole*, a film directed by Billy Wilder based on the real-life
story of Floyd Collins.

Desny did not sue for copyright infringement. Indeed,
Desny merely pitched an idea, and ideas are not protectable under copyright law (although he did have a sixty-five-
page treatment, Wilder's secretary told him not to send it,
as Wilder would not read it). Instead, Desny sued for
breach of a contract that he claimed was *implied* between
him and Wilder/Paramount; namely, that if they used his
idea and story synopsis, they would pay him the reasonable value of their use.

In 1956, the Supreme Court of California upheld Mr.
Desny's claim, and the concept of idea theft was born.
Ever since, producers and production companies have
adopted the policy of not accepting unsolicited material
from people not represented by agents or lawyers. Standard industry practice is not to accept unsolicited story
material from unknown people unless they sign a waiver

that stipulates they will not subsequently sue the company or individuals receiving the material.

The precedent established by the *Desny v. Wilder* case continues to have an effect. When someone meets with a producer, studio executive, or other purchaser of literary material, state law in at least California and New York recognizes that an implied contract exists, and that the person conveying the story (even if it's "only" an idea) is doing so in order to sell his or her material or to get hired to develop a screenplay.

The scope of an implied contract is broader and potentially more powerful than the protection given under copyright. An implied contract covers the full spec script, not just those portions that are protected by copyright.[4] So it is important to understand that copyright is not the *only* way to protect your creative work.

What is the implied contract in a pitch meeting? If you pitch ideas to me, and if I use one of your ideas, then I will pay you the reasonable value.

conveyance + use = payment

Conveyance is relatively easy to prove. But *use* is problematic, as we discuss and analyze in detail in the "Substantial Similarity" section of chapter 5, "Copyright Infringement." (Indeed, not to plant a plot-spoiler, but whether or not you have a case will turn on whether you're able to convincingly show *use*.)

For another famous case of idea theft case, see the section on *Coming to America* in chapter 7, "Confessions of an Expert Witness."

RELEASE FORMS: SIGNING (OR NOT SIGNING) RELEASES

Unless you have an agent or someone else who can get you directly "into the room" to meet in person with potential buyers, you'll probably have to make contact indirectly by mail or e-mail. But before the potential buyer will take receipt of your spec, they'll most likely ask you to sign a release form.

The release form declares that your signature evidences you agree to a contract with the other side in which you give up your right to sue if you think they have stolen something from your spec.

So, not surprisingly, one of the questions that we're most frequently asked is, "They want me to sign a release, but it's so one-sided in their favor that it's practically unconscionable. Should I still sign?"

Sign only if "they" are trustworthy industry professionals.

The release that you'll be asked to sign will be very one-sided in favor of the person or company requiring your signature. The release was prepared by the buyer's lawyer solely for the buyer's protection. And that's usually at the expense of your rights.

Indeed, the typical release will say that you "acknowledge and agree" that the production company looks at innumerable different projects, that it has many projects already in development, that there is a small and finite number of story plots, that the company may already have a project similar to yours in development, and that in consideration for reading your spec you release the company from any and all liability and will not sue.

The general rule of contract law is that you are bound by what you sign. Most people have become comfortable with the notion that one-sided releases we can't and don't negotiate are unenforceable. They're pure boilerplate. They're printed on the back of valet parking receipts. They're unconscionable!

Unconscionability is a legal defense that was developed in the context of consumer purchases and arose from the consumer protection movement in the 1970s. But there has never been a published opinion testing the merits of unconscionability as a defense in an entertainment industry context regarding a boilerplate release for a spec script. We suspect that it would be a losing position.

Two elements must exist for unconscionability to be found:

· Unequal bargaining power. Really unequal. David-and-Goliath inequality.

· The transaction is necessary. Not just wanted, but needed. That means it is a necessity of life.

In the spec script context, you have the first element, *but probably not the second.* No one is forcing you to do a deal with this particular producer or production company.

Again, no published opinion has ever applied this doctrine in an entertainment business context. Perhaps someday a court will apply the unconscionability doctrine to a spec release form. But you probably don't want to be the writer who shoulders the financial and emotional burden of bringing such a law-changing suit.

So how do you get your spec read? How indeed.

Knowing that the one-sided release may well be enforceable should give a writer pause and make them think about who is behind the release. Are you dealing with a reputable studio or production company? Are they well-known professionals with an established reputation in the industry? Or is this an unknown or fledgling producer?

We suggest that your due diligence should be placed not so much on the text of the release (which you can't negotiate or otherwise control), but instead on the person/entity behind the release (you can control who you decided to show your spec to).

Ultimately, there are only two things that you can do with an egregiously one-sided release:

· shrug and sign, knowing that no one will buy your spec if no one is reading your spec, and that this is a reputable reader and not someone who is likely to steal your stuff, or

· don't sign and walk away, because you don't know or don't trust this particular would-be reader.

The choice is yours. Just make that choice knowing that the form might well be a release from liability.

PITCHING

What is a pitch? A concise oral presentation of an idea, yes. But it's more.

Pitching is not something you do to try and get work. Pitching *is* work.

That is, pitching is a professional service.[5] You, the writer, are performing the service of bringing ideas to the—

attention of a producer. In theory, you could get paid for the service of pitching, but the entertainment industry hasn't developed that way. There are too many sellers/ writers and far too few buyers/producers. The buyers/producers don't need to pay for it! So pitching is the free service that you perform to see if your idea is useable. In the parlance of business, pitching is your "loss leader."

Every pitch meeting can be considered an implied-in-fact contact. The potential buyer has invited you to the meeting to hear your pitches, and to pass your projects up the ladder to persons with "green light" or purchase authority, if the projects merit such consideration. You have come to the meeting for the express purposes of pitching projects to sell. The context is commercial, not social.

We create films for different personal reasons, but our common denominator is that we want to reach an audience. To do that, we usually have to sell others on the merits of our project. Sell it to investors. Sell it to a producer, a director, to actors. Then we sell the finished product to a distributor. Ultimately, we sell it to the audience.

But is pitching safe from a legal standpoint? More particularly, if I'm pitching my project around town, can't someone simply take it from me?

Ideas are free for the taking unless and until someone promises to do something, or not do something, with them. And that promise can be expressed in a written non-disclosure agreement or implied by the context of a pitch meeting.

Idea theft as we know it didn't exist—or at least didn't exist as a cause of action—in the golden studio era (roughly from the late 1920s through the 1940s) of screenwriting. Sure, maybe writers stole from other writers. But the studios most certainly did not steal from writers. Why? Because the studios paid for all intellectual property right up front. The writers were all studio employees under contract. As such, writers had no expectation of ownership in their writing. Instead, writers expected a weekly paycheck. This check was tied to their status as employees, not to their output and authorship per se.

As the world shifted to an independent contractor model in the wake of federal antitrust litigation and a settlement, or consent decree, that went into effect in 1948, a writer's compensation became tied to authorship rather than a studio employment contract. No authorship, no compensation.

Ultimately, the risk of idea theft from pitching comes down to who you're dealing with. Are they reputable? Reputable means a repeat player who is in the business of purchasing material for use, rather than someone who is trolling for ideas that they themselves can then take to a reputable player.

There is a tension on both sides of the table, between studios that claim ideas are a dime a dozen but nevertheless are always on the lookout for them, and writers who think their ideas are protectable but don't make enough effort to protect them.

Pitching Only an Idea

We are often asked if pitching an idea, rather than a completed screenplay, is a good idea. After all, there are published books and articles that suggest you can sell mere ideas on a pitch. Often, the person asking us about pitching-ideas-sans-writing confesses that they aren't sure they have the time or ability to write an actual script.

Our advice is always "Don't."

The amount of money you are likely to receive for a story idea is going to be minuscule, especially in comparison to the amount a completed screenplay might fetch.

If you do manage to get paid for an idea, where does that leave your career? You pitched an idea? Will someone *hire* you to come up with others? Not likely—they'll wait until you have another idea, and if they like it, they'll pay you a minuscule amount of money for that one too.

What we advise people with ideas to do is *write the script*.

If you're not willing to invest the time and energy needed to bring a screenplay to fruition, then your chances of having a creative career in film or television are not very good. You have to prove not only that you have ideas, but that you know how to express them in a completed work.

Pitches and Leave-Behinds

If you get the opportunity to pitch your idea, should you leave behind a treatment, screenplay, or some other writing?

There are arguments for both sides of this question. Our belief is that yes, you should leave behind something, and generally it should be a completed script.

What is the purpose of a pitch? Although sometimes pitches result in a sale during the meeting itself, this is an exceptional event. Furthermore, what is it that is sold? The words you spoke during the meeting? The treatment or script you were prepared to leave behind but which the production company now buys without bothering to read? Or perhaps they buy the rights to the script you have yet to write. Or maybe it's just an option. In any case, it is naive to expect they will directly purchase what is in your pitch, especially if you are not already established.

The main purpose of a pitch is not to make a sale on the spot. It is to cause the people who hear your pitch to lean forward as you describe your story and at least implicitly say "Tell me more." The "more" here is ultimately going to be found in the script.

The Writers Guild of America disapproves of the practice of leaving behind material a member has written, reasoning that this constitutes giving away your work for free. This may be true for experienced WGA members, whose prior work attests to their ability to perform. But if you're not a guild member and are at an early stage of your career, where potential employers have no means of judging your abilities other than the brief discussion they've had with you during the pitch meeting, leaving behind written material may help convince them that they should continue talking to you about your project or perhaps even other projects.

What's in a Good Pitch

It is important to understand that in the vast majority of cases, your pitch will have to be repitched after you leave the room. The junior executive whose job it is to filter out all but the most promising projects will pitch it to their boss. Then the boss will pitch it to *their* boss, and on up the ladder.

If you are at an early stage in your career, you will not pitch to anyone who has the power to green-light, or approve, your project. You will almost certainly pitch to junior executives, many younger than you. At the end of the day, their immediate boss will ask them, "What good pitches did you hear today?"

If the person you originally pitched to has trouble remembering important details from your pitch, they are not likely to mention your story for fear of looking foolish. This fact helps reveal that a good pitch must be vivid, succinct, and memorable.

If the story pitched isn't vivid, it makes little impression and will therefore be hard to summarize for others. If the pitch isn't succinct, extremely busy people (such as those who make decisions) will not have the patience to continue listening. And if the original pitch isn't memorable, the higher-up person who must, in turn, be able to pass it on to others will not care or be able to do so.

CHAPTER FIVE

Copyright Infringement

PRACTICAL CONSIDERATIONS

Stop us if this story is your story:

You're looking for a film to watch. You're skimming through the new releases. But then you stop abruptly. At first, you don't believe your eyes. It's *your* title. That is to say, the title of a new release is the title of your most resent unsold spec. You look closer. You read the story blurb. It's familiar, much too familiar. Your mouth feels dry. You read the credits. It takes a moment, but then you recognize a name. The credited writer's name. *It's not your name.* It's the contact person at a start-up production company that was soliciting spec screenplays about a year ago. You'd sent them your spec. You feel sick to your stomach. The story is yours.

Many questions race through your mind: Do I have any legal recourse? If I pursue this, what lies ahead? Should I sue?

This chapter focuses primarily on the first question—whether you have a good *legal* claim. But before we get into that, let's frame the discussion within the *practicalities*.

Even if you have a good claim, there are many valid reasons for deciding not to pursue it.

Public War of Attrition/Private Settlement

There are two operative realities to idea theft and copyright infringement disputes:

- Litigation is a war of attrition, and
- If you manage to weather the litigation storm and survive to the point when it seems more likely than not that you—the actual writer—are going to win, then the defendants will offer to settle by paying you under the umbrella of a private non-disclosure agreement.

Research shows that in the last twenty-five years, only one out of over fifty copyright infringement cases in the Ninth Circuit has resulted in a win for the writer.[1] And it has been estimated that the average cost of a copyright dispute over a film—from filing the complaint all the way through trial by jury—is $1.5 million per party.

In short, the odds are stacked against you as an aggrieved screenwriter, and it is extremely expensive to go the distance.

This is a dismal picture of litigation. And we wouldn't want to mislead you by painting a pretty one. But is it the complete picture? We may have an epistemological problem that skews the odds. Because we don't know what we don't know.

We certainly know what's in the public record—that is, what's required to be published into the public record as a matter of law or accessible in the official court files. That means the public filing of lawsuits, filings in the trial court record during the course of litigation, any memoranda of decision at the end of the trial court case, and, if the trail court decision is appealed, any published court opinions from the appellate court. But cases are rarely appealed. Indeed, many cases never go the full distance in the trial courts. Many are settled by the parties prior to trial, and some are simply dismissed very early as being completely without merit.

We learn about unpublished matters to the extent that the parties involved or colleagues tell us about them or the press covers the story. But otherwise, we only know about the cases that are published, and even then, only about the portions of those case that are published.

We may not know about any of the following:

pre-lawsuit settlements (i.e., a writer sends a demand letter and the parties resolve their differences prior to any lawsuit being filed);

pre-trial settlements (i.e., a lawsuit has been filed and is under way but has not yet reached trial);

post-judgment/appeal pending settlement (i.e., it's not over until it's over—as the case is posturing on appeal the parties may [again] talk settlement);

appeals that aren't certified for publication (i.e., there's no settlement and the appellate court issues an "unpublished opinion," which remains in the public record and is accessible on the court's web page for a very short time [30 days, typically], and is only binding on the parties to that particular case; the unpublished opinion cannot be cited as law by other parties in other lawsuits);

settlement after remand but before a new trial (i.e., the appellate court finds errors and sends the case back down to the trial court for retrial; the parties very often settle at this juncture rather than litigating further now that they have the added benefit of insight from the appellate court);

published appeals that were remanded back to the trial court for further proceedings that were then not published.

You get the idea. But back to the more meaningful questions: Can you afford a lawsuit? Monetarily? Emotionally? Will litigation do your professional career any good? Will litigation do your mental health any good?

Writer's don't sue (just) for money. They sue for something much more precious: vindication.

What will this lawsuit mean to forward movement in your career? In your life? Do you have the time to fight rather than create? Or if you don't fight, will it freeze you from any further creation?

Only you can answer those questions for yourself. But we can help you answer the more fundamental threshold question: Do you have a case?

COPYRIGHT INFRINGEMENT:
THE PRIMA FACIE CASE

Certainly it comes as no surprise that, ultimately, you must prove your case in court.

But long before you *prove* your case in court, you must sufficiently *plead* your case on the page. Indeed, if you can't first make your case on the page, you'll never get the opportunity to make your case from the witness stand in open court.

Prima facie is about pleadings on the page. "Prima facie" is a legal term of art. Taken from the Latin *prīmus* (first) and *faciēs* (face), the phrase translates to "on its face; at first appearance; at first view before investigation."

In legalese, a prima facie showing is one that is sufficient to establish a case unless disproved. That means that when we read your allegations—and we assume for argument's sake that your allegations are all true—you have stated the requisite elements for an actionable claim. In other words, you indeed have a case.[2]

So what are the required elements for a prima facie case of copyright infringement? There are only two: ownership and copying. That is, you must show that you actually own the underlying work (usually very easy), and that someone else copied it without your permission (usually very difficult).

Copyright infringement can be accidental or careless (i.e., negligent) as well as intentional.[3] The infringer's intentions are irrelevant. Copyright infringement is a strict liability tort.[4]

The devil is in the details. Please read on.

OWNERSHIP

The first prima facie element of a claim for copyright infringement is ownership. That is, your ownership of your script is the threshold element of your claim. After all, if you don't actually own your script, then you have nothing to complain about. Or, as the courts say, you have "no standing" to bring a lawsuit.

How do you show—that is, *evidence*—your ownership? Well, let's start at the beginning. Where did your story come from? Do you have a document trail—paper or electronic—of your development process? Do you have research notes from any public domain materials you relied on? Drafts of your outline(s), beat sheet(s), first draft, as well as all subsequent drafts? All of this is useful evidence to show that your story came from you; that *you* are the author and owner.

Now, as you probably know, you do not need to register anything with anyone to have a valid copyright in material you write. Your rights attach at the moment of tangible creation. But before you can bring a lawsuit for copyright infringement, you must file an application for copyright registration with the United States Copyright Office.[5] And the Copyright Office must have accepted your application before you sue. If you bring a lawsuit without first obtaining proper copyright registration, the court will dismiss your lawsuit, and it will not permit you to refile unless and until you obtain and submit proof of registration.[6]

Does that mean that copyright registration is conclusive proof of your ownership? No, of course not. When the Copyright Office issues a certificate of registration to you, the certificate merely confirms that you have completed the application form, deposited a copy of the material, and paid the required fee.

The Copyright Office examines your application on its face, treating all the statements as true, but it does not examine or investigate to determine the actual truth or merits of the underlying statements in your application. The result of this is that copyright registration only gives you a prima facie showing of ownership. Someone could still challenge your ownership with admissible evidence to the contrary to rebut your prima facie showing. But unless someone does so, you are the prima facie owner if you are the registered copyright owner.

Bottom line: Copyright registration is a necessary prerequisite to your bringing a claim for copyright ownership in court, but it is not enough to conclusively establish your ownership. In addition to a registration certificate, you should have a *document trail* of your development process, showing when and how your story was created and evolved, from idea to draft(s) to final. Save your working notes and materials. Save your various drafts. Don't delete anything.

Chronology Is Not Causality

Unfortunately, it is all too easy for a creative person to conclude (mistakenly) that because they created something, and someone else created something similar *afterward*, the subsequent creator must have stolen it from them. But it is a logical fallacy that if one thing follows another, it must have been caused by the first. The subsequent work might be the result of copying, or it simply might be the result of independent creation.

In Latin, this logical fallacy is referred to as *post hoc ergo propter hoc* ("after this, therefore because of this").

While it is critical that you show that your work was first-in-time, you also will have to separately establish evidence of actual copying.

COPYING

The second prima facie element of a claim for copyright infringement is *copying.*

In technical terms, "copying" is shorthand for the infringing of any of the copyright owner's exclusive rights as described in the Copyright Act.[7] For writers, that usually means the rights to reproduce (copy directly), to distribute (publish or exhibit), and to prepare derivative works (sequel, prequel, and merchandising).

That someone copied your script without your permission is the heart of your claim. After all, if no one actually copied from your script, then you have not been wronged. Once again, you have "no standing" to sue.

So how do you show evidence of copying?

Direct Proof

There is seldom, if ever, direct evidence of copying.

Direct evidence is direct proof of a fact, such as testimony by an eyewitness or participant about what they personally saw or heard or did.[8] It's unlikely that you'll find an eyewitness who saw copying taking place as it happened. No one ever gets caught in the act of copying. And it would be unusual for someone to admit or confess that they copied from you.

So how can you prove copying when there is no direct evidence? With indirect evidence, which is more commonly referred to as "circumstantial evidence."

Circumstantial Evidence

Circumstantial evidence is evidence that requires some reasoning to prove a fact.

For example, if you wake up this morning and see a wet sidewalk, you may conclude from that observed fact that it rained during the night. But other evidence, such as the existence of an automatic sprinkler system or a broken fire hydrant, may offer a different explanation. Circumstantial evidence would be using an observed fact (wet sidewalk) to prove another fact by reasoning (rained last night). Before a jury decides that a fact has been proven by circumstantial evidence, it must consider all the evidence in the light of reason, experience, and common sense.[9]

A common misconception is that circumstantial evidence is somehow less worthy than direct evidence. Maybe this misperception comes from police dramas, where defense attorneys will balk at accusations against their clients by retorting, "That's just circumstantial." Perhaps. But in actuality, the law makes no distinction between the weight to be given to either direct or circumstantial evidence.[10] One can be as persuasive as the other.

In copyright infringement cases, circumstantial evidence is proof of certain facts (access and substantial similarity) to prove another fact (copying) by reasoning. That is,

Access + Substantial Similarity = Copying

ACCESS

Access is defined as an "opportunity to view or copy another's work."[11]

Opportunity is "more than a bare possibility," in the sense that most anything is possible.[12] You need more than mere speculation or conjecture. You must show that there was a reasonable possibility that the filmmakers viewed your spec. We think of opportunity as consisting of both timing and connection or nexus.

Timing

Your spec must be first-in-time. That is, your spec must have been physically in existence before the filmmakers finished their film, otherwise, it would have been chronologically impossible for them to copy your script in making their film.

A central benefit of WGA registration is that it establishes an objective and clear date for when your script came into existence. For more about this, please see chapter 6, "Copyright Fundamentals."

So let's say you have a WGA registration that shows that your script was first-in-time. So far so good. But you need more.

Connection or Nexus

You must construct a plausible connection between your spec and the filmmakers. Although each case involving the question of access presents its own unique facts, there are two categorical approaches. A sufficient connection or nexus is shown where either of the following exists:

Chain of events. A particular chain of events connecting your spec and the film, such as a pitch meeting or other dealings involving a manager, agent, production company, development executive, or other such intermediary, or even the filmmakers themselves; or

Widely disseminated. Your work has been widely disseminated to the public.[13]

For most spec writers, we are talking about the first prong, chain of events. The second prong traditionally applies to commercially published novelists.[14]

But that's so twentieth century. What about in the internet age? Although the internet has the power to reach a wide and diverse audience, web publication does not necessarily constitute wide dissemination.[15] Millennial readers would agree, we're sure. Individual web publications are lost in an undifferentiated mass of data in cyberspace unless and until something drives an audience to them. Dissemination is a function of your placement on search engines.

How Could the Filmmakers Have Seen Your Script?

Did you pitch your script to the filmmaker? Did you show or give them a copy? Did your agent, or manager, or lawyer? Did your writing partner, or life partner, or angry ex–life partner? You must ask yourself who had access to your script. Make a list. Then see if you can connect these intermediaries to the filmmakers.

Was your script publicly accessible, say, through a screenwriting competition? Was it listed on a studio or production company "tracking board"? Or a web site?

You must connect the dots. Access is a continuum. The continuum must start with your script pre-dating their film, and it must end with the actual creative team that made the film having seen your script. You must connect each and every dot on the continuum.

Writers often can trace getting their spec to the filmmaker's production company, or as the case law refers to it, "corporate receipt." But often the trail ends there. The writer is not able to show that once it was within the company, the spec actually found its way to the filmmakers themselves. You need some proof that the particular creative team for the project at the company saw your spec.[16]

The key is knowing the identity of intermediary persons. You must show you submitted your spec to an intermediary who was in a position to transmit it to the filmmakers. The intermediary can be a person who has supervisory responsibility for the film, contributed ideas and materials to the film, or worked in the same company unit as the filmmakers.[17]

You should have a record showing who you gave or pitched your spec to, and who that person intended to give or pitch your spec to. Diligent professional writers always have a record of with whom they've talked or to whom they've shown their specs.

The chain of purchasing or creative command may already be somewhat accessible without your directly asking. Look at the organizational chart on the web page or in corporate filings. If you're using an agent, discuss with them (ideally, in advance of submission) your desire to know the names of intermediaries and decision makers.

But after your initial meeting in the pitch room, will you know with any specificity who will see the spec next? Who will the person you pitched talk to when the project moves up the chain of command?

If names or title are volunteered, then most definitely take note. But if not, you probably shouldn't ask, because—unfortunately—the person you're meeting with may not be taking your spec anywhere. After all, the entertainment biz convention is to never say "no." This is also known as the "Hollywood yes."

That is, the person you're meeting with will only say nice things—encouraging things—that sound like prequels to "yes," even if they're ultimately going to pass. They won't tell you if they're not interested in the story. Not in the room, that is. So even if there's no intention to pitch your project up the chain, they certainly won't tell you that. They don't want to have to explain their decision, and they don't want you to push for an explanation.

Ultimately, do you need to have an ironclad, absolutely positive showing of access? No. But you do need to show a chain of facts *that make it more likely than not* that the filmmakers had an opportunity to use your spec.

The bottom line is that you should do what you can to protect yourself. But remember, first and foremost: you're trying to sell, not prepare for litigation.

STRIKING SIMILARITY

What if you cannot show any connection or nexus what-soever between your spec and someone else's film? There just is no trail to connect the dots. Do you lose? Probably. But not necessarily. There is still one very slight chance left: striking similarity. If certain elements in their film are "strikingly similar" to elements in your spec, this will give rise to an inference of copying.[18]

Striking similarity means that the accused work is so highly similar to yours that it *could not possibly* have been the result of independent creation.[19] The striking similarity may go to just certain portions or elements of the two works, or it can go to the two works in total. Obviously, the more elements there are that are strikingly similar, the more it appears that one was copied from the other.

A finding of striking similarity puts the inference in your favor, but the filmmakers could rebut that inference. For example, they might show that their film was com-pleted before your spec was started. That would make copying impossible, and that would rebut the finding of striking similarity. In that case the striking similarity must be a coincidence, or because you both used a common source, but not the result of copying.[20] A film could very well be original and non-infringing even though it closely resembles your spec.

The equation cuts both ways:

Access	Similarity	Possible Conclusion
0%	75%+	Striking Similarity
0%	75%+	Independent Development

We pick 75 percent by way of example only—because it's a convenient midpoint between 50 and 100 percent—and not as a strict rule of mathematical certainty. Similarity is a continuum, and you must have a very high degree of it to raise the issue of striking similarity. A similarity of 100 percent would indicate verbatim copying or photocopying and would be essentially impossible for the alleged infringers to rebut with a showing of purported independent development.[21]

We want to put the doctrine of substantial similarity in its proper and very limited context. Striking similarity is so extremely rare that we were tempted to omit it from this book. (But we included it because exceptional situations are the ones that seem to fascinate people most and often lead to confusion or bad cocktail-party talk.)

There are absolutely no published Ninth Circuit cases in which a writer has prevailed using a striking similarity theory.

Indeed, between the two of us, in our collective eighty-plus years of copyright experience, we've only seen striking similarity once in each of our careers. And, coincidentally, it involved the same case! (We were each independently consulted by the same writer; we'll omit identifiers to preserve confidentiality.) In that case, the spec and the shooting script were scene-for-scene, page-for-page, and almost word-for-word identical, except for the renaming of characters and the occasional minor and insubstantial edits to dialogue. The copying was just short of photocopying. Now that's striking!

We mention that case because the writer had lost a laptop and had no other written record of where their spec had been submitted, so there was no plausible way to prove access. They mistakenly thought this precluded their claim. Not so.

But unless you have striking similarity, which is highly unlikely, you will need to establish some degree of access.

SUBSTANTIAL SIMILARITY

How substantially similar is your work to the (allegedly) infringing film? That is *the* question. Indeed, the issue of substantial similarity is the single most significant factor in determining whether you have a good case.

Substantial similarity is the big battleground. Some would argue that it is the only battleground. If you cannot show substantial similarity, you cannot win. Fade out, end of story. You cannot win on any theory of recovery: not on copyright infringement, not on implied contract/idea theft, not on implied contract/non-disclosure, not on any theory at all.

Why? Because the existence of substantial similarity is, in effect, the key (circumstantial) evidence that your script was *used*. If you can't prove that your script was actually used, there was no copying and you lose.

The substantial similarity test involves the judge and jury comparing your script to the other party's script(s) and/or film. But this is where most writers get confused about their chances of winning.

You may think your chances are better than they actually are. Why? Because the comparison is not simply between their film and your script. It is something less.

Filtering First, Comparison Second

The court compares their film to *only the protectable portions of your script.*[22] Unprotected elements in your script are irrelevant. Before your script can be compared to their film, the unprotected elements must be identified and filtered out from consideration.[23]

This recalls our discussion back in chapter 1, "Free for the Taking." Elements that are free for your use without restriction are also free for everyone else in the world to use without restriction. No one has a protected property interest in them.

So What Gets Filtered Out before Comparison?

Story elements that are *factual* (news, history, true biography) or *functional* (*scènes à faire*, stock characters) are excluded as non-copyrightable.[24] Whatever remains is yours. Whatever remains is your protected expression. Whatever remains is now ready for the substantial similarity comparison.

Various circuit courts of the United States Circuit Court of Appeals apply somewhat different methods to test for substantial similarity. If you're a screenwriter, you're probably working in California (Ninth Circuit) or New York (Second Circuit). Even if you don't work in either place, chances are that you'll be trying to sell your material in Hollywood, which means California. So it should come as no surprise that most of the published opinions addressing screenplays and copyright infringement come out of California and the Ninth Circuit Court of Appeals.

The Ninth Circuit uses a two-part test for substantial similarity. That test consists of an extrinsic analysis done by the judge, and then, if you get past the judge, an intrinsic analysis done by the jury. In most—indeed, almost all—of the published Ninth Circuit opinions, the aggrieved screenwriter was *not* able to get past the judge, and therefore never made it to a jury of peers. The studios typically will not entertain settlement discussions until after the claim has been tested by the judge, and only if the screenwriter gets past the judge on the extrinsic analysis.

So how is the substantial similarity test applied?

EXTRINSIC TEST: ISOLATING ELEMENTS

The extrinsic test is an objective test based on specific expressive elements. The number and actual elements themselves aren't as important as is the concept that this is an objective test intended to isolate and compare elements.[25] The analysis is done by the judge alone, with the use of expert witness testimony at the judge's discretion.

The extrinsic test is where most copyright infringement cases end, one way or the other. If the filmmakers win, then the court dismisses the case. But if the writer wins, then the filmmakers (almost) always settle out of court, before the case can proceed to a jury. This tactic is based on the belief that judges are educated, analytical, and rational, whereas juries are somewhat uneducated, emotional, and irrational. Perhaps. At any rate, if you can't get past the judge, you can't get to the jury. But if you do get past the judge, then the jury is probably going to be a much easier audience to convince.

Copyright infringement claims against motion picture studios and television networks are fiercely uphill battles for writers. During the last three decades, studios and networks have almost universally prevailed on pre-trial dispositive motions called "motions for summary judgment."[26] These cases never reach the jury.

The extrinsic test focuses on "articulable similarities between the plot, themes, dialog[ue], mood, setting, pace, characters, and sequence of events."[27]

This oft-quoted phrase is the mantra recited for forty-plus years by courts in the Ninth Circuit embarking on the extrinsic test for a substantial similarity analysis. The courts will isolate and compare each element, one by one.[28] And that's what we'll do in the pages that follow.

1. Plot

Plot is story. Indeed, a typical dictionary definition of "plot" is "the plan or main story."

Other definitions of "plot" sound like physical metaphors for story: (1) a small area of planted ground, (2) a small piece of land in a cemetery, (3) a measured piece of land, (4) a secret plan for accomplishing a (usually evil or unlawful) goal. Apt metaphors for your story, yes? Your story as your place in the world—it's what you plant, it's what you leave behind when you're gone. It's your movement from plan to goal.

Are there any truly new plots? Plot is the element most susceptible to being filtered out from the substantial similarity analysis and not considered because of *scènes à faire*. That is to say, your plot may not be yours, at least not completely. There are a limited number of plot structures, and they've been around for a long, long time.[29] A few courts discuss plot and sequence of events as closely related concepts.[30] Remember that we are speaking in the legal context of a substantial similarity analysis. Most courts treat plot and story as synonymous.

But writers, and especially those familiar with E. M. Forster's *Aspects of the Novel*, understand that story is mere chronology, whereas plot is chronology as well as causality.[31] If you're a UCLA School of Theater, Film and Television alum, you may have been instructed that "plot is physical events; story is emotional events."[32] Although these distinctions may be useful in helping you write your story, they are not distinctions recognized by the law or by any of the courts.

Indeed, you'll note that story is not even an element in the Ninth Circuit's substantial similarity test. That means that for purposes of determining substantial similarity, the element of plot must include all—physical events and emotional events as well their chronology and causality.

In our view, plot is what happens; story is why it happens. But for copyright law purposes, plot is story.

2. Theme(s)

What is theme?

For copyright infringement purposes, theme is probably the least significant of the substantial similarity elements. Why? Because theme tends to be general and somewhat abstract. Themes, by their very nature, tend to sound simple and trite. Many, many films share the same or a similar theme. This means that you're probably not the first to explore "your" theme. Any given theme probably has been done before (*Avatar*) and before (*Dances with Wolves*) and before (*Pocahontas*) and before (*The Iliad*).

Discussions of theme always bring us back to seventh-grade literature class (e.g., mankind versus nature, good versus evil). That's a move toward abstractions. And that's a move in the wrong direction.

Dictionary definitions, and at least one published legal case, suggest that theme is "the subject or topic of artistic expression, a point of view embodied upon in a work of art, or even . . . the 'unifying or dominant idea' inherent in a given work."[33] So theme is subject, along with your particular opinion on the subject. Or, if you prefer a formula:

Subject + Your Opinion = Theme

For example—

Life (subject) is wonderful (opinion).

Love (subject) sucks (opinion).

Marriage (subject) is better the second time around (opinion).

You see the approach. What's your script's theme? You've likely explored and answered this question during your writing, rewriting, and pitching.

3. Dialogue

Dialogue is words.

Dialogue is the words written down the middle of the page in a script for characters to speak. Dialogue is the words spoken by the actors in a film. There is no ambiguity about what constitutes dialogue.

Dialogue is the most *tangible* form of expression, and as such, it is the most *traceable* form of expression. Certainly no infringer is foolish enough to steal dialogue word for word. But in the absence of such verbatim copying, it is difficult to establish substantial similarity. Indeed, no published opinion exists where a court has found substantial similarity regarding this element.

In a few cases where dialect or use of technical terminology has, at a first blush, given the appearance of similarity, the courts have gone on to decide that such similarity is a result of both works being set in the same milieu or subculture (e.g., the underground world of competitive poker).[34]

This is kind of like applying the *scènes à faire* doctrine to speech. A particular milieu or subculture will have its own terminology or slang. Just because your script and someone else's film use the same terminology or slang in dialogue does not necessarily mean that the filmmakers have copied from you.[35] It could just mean that you're both attuned to the vernacular of that particular world.

A few courts discuss dialogue in conjunction with other elements, such as character[36] or mood.[37] These elements are less literary and more cinematographic. And that's a step in the right direction.

4. Mood

Mood is feeling. Mood is the dominant emotion or prevailing attitude.

Some courts combine the discussion of mood into a troika of mood, setting, and pace.[38] Others make a combined duet of mood and pace[39] or mood and setting.[40] One published opinion has combined mood with dialogue.[41] Another has combined it with tone and feeling,[42] though that really is a tautology, since mood is synonymous with tone and feeling.

Indeed, mood is the element most likely to be combined by the courts with something else. Perhaps that is because the courts are grappling with an understanding of what constituent parts of a film actually create the overall mood.

Certainly pace is a central method of conveying mood (i.e., comedy is fast, drama is slower). But pace is not the only method. Music is another central element (i.e., mood music). So is color (bright versus dark; full palette versus limited palette).

5. Setting

Setting is place (geographical and physical locations) and time (past, present, future; day or night).

But be careful. Does your spec have unusual or unique physical settings? Does it at least have a definite geographic location? Common settings such as houses, front yards, offices, restaurants, and car interiors are quite generic and do not offer any copyrightable expression.[43]

This is one of those situations where there is tension between what may be advisable from a legal standpoint and what may be advisable from a business standpoint.

From a legal standpoint, more specificity means more copyright protection. But from a business standpoint, you may be inclined to write your low- or no-budget spec with a generic location so that you don't (inadvertently) drive up the budget by "demanding" certain pricey locations. Your (smarter) instinct may be to write to no particular location at all, so that the producer has the broadest latitude in deciding where to shoot the film. And that's a good business strategy. Just be aware that your generic locations won't support your claim in an infringement dispute.

The ideal reconciliation of this tension between copyright protection and business concerns is to write very specific and unique locations, but ones that are easily or inexpensively replicated. Now that takes creativity!

Setting is more than just another prop. *Protectable* setting should also be more like a character.

Setting should play a role in the plot and contribute to the thematic content. The setting should be part of the catalyst for the changes, development, and growth in your protagonist's character arc.[44]

6. Pace

Pace is speed: the rate of movement, performance, and delivery. Tempo.

Some courts combine the discussion of pace into a troika of mood, setting, and pace.[45] Others make a combined duet of pace and mood.[46]

As we opined earlier in the context of mood, certainly pace is a central method of conveying mood (i.e., comedy is fast, drama is slower). But think of the relationship between pace and mood like this: pace is a cause; mood is the effect or result.

7. *Characters / Character Interaction*

Characters are characters, but not all are created equal.

Some are mere stock characters or character types, and these are given very little copyright protection. Indeed, the details that make characters memorable are the same ones that render them protectable: unique details and "sufficiently distinctive" elements.[47]

Copyright protection is given to characters who are especially distinctive and are "sufficiently delineated" and display "consistent, widely identifiable traits."[48] Think James Bond,[49] Rocky,[50] Godzilla,[51] Batman,[52] even the Batmobile.[53]

A few older cases talk about character interaction as an element separate from character. But how does character interaction differ from character? Aren't they one and the same? Yes, probably.

In film, characters are defined by actions—their own actions, or the reactions of other characters to them. As an audience, we know a character by what we see them do (or not do), by what we hear them say (or not say), by the way that they do or say something (or not), and by what others say or do in reaction to the character. For all practical purposes, in film, interaction is action. Characters do not have characteristics until they act or refrain from acting.

This is not necessarily true in literature, where characters can live mostly in their heads. A literary character can have a rich internal monologue that never manifests itself in external interaction. The true inner self is never revealed to the public. Look to nineteenth-century Russian novels for examples.

But if we had to differentiate character interaction from character, we would look to the unique elements that exist in the first few minutes of a film—the set stage elements, if you will. We would ask ourselves, what is the character's place in the world? Does the character have any unique physical traits? And perhaps most significantly, how do these set-stage traits contribute to the story ahead? Do they do so in a way that is unique?

8. Sequence of Events

The earliest legal cases referred to this element simply as sequence, but that soon became sequence of events.[54]

How is sequence of events different from plot? The two are not necessarily different, especially if the plot moves forward in time with "chronological legitimacy." That is, things happen in a forward-moving continuum just as they do in real life (i.e., 1:00 comes before 2:00, Monday before Tuesday, January before February). The chronology is straightforward.

But plot and sequence of events are not necessarily the same either. In some films—*Pulp Fiction* and *Memento* and *500 Days of Summer,* to name just a few—the plot may be presented out of sequence. That is to say, the narrative violates straight chronology.

Sequence of events is the forward-moving narrative. It is narrative playing forward from page-to-page in the script or from moment-to-moment on the screen.

9. *Other Elements?*

As we've seen, the extrinsic test for substantial similarity considers certain very specific expressive elements: "articulable similarities between the plot, themes, dialog[ue], mood, setting, pace, characters, and sequence of events."[55] But is this list exclusive? Or may the court consider other elements too?

No court has addressed this question squarely yet. When the list of elements was originally developed, the court's wording strongly suggested a non-exclusive list (i.e., "[t]he criteria in *this* case might include *such* characteristics of a written work *as* plot, theme, [etc.]" [emphasis added]).[56] And several courts have reiterated the substantial similarity test with similar non-exclusive-sounding language.[57] Most courts, though, drop the "such as" similitude language and instead seem to state a finite list. Is this deliberate? Again, it is unclear because the question has not yet been addressed by any court.

If the eight-element list is not exhaustive or exclusive, then what other elements would we consider?

Courts and copyright lawyers pay the most attention to the things that they themselves know how to use: words. These copyright infringement cases are not so much about the film as about the script. But what about unique elements in direction, editing, photography, lighting, music, computer-generated imagery, and so on?

We suppose that the operative question is to what extent these (cinematic) elements are captured in the (literary) elements already included in the courts' eight-element test. And that question probably is best addressed, as the courts are apt to say, on a case-by-case basis.

But we do know of at least one additional element that has come onto the courts' radar: title.

10. Title

Title is *not* included in the Ninth Circuit's mantra of elements used for a substantial similarity comparison. But the Ninth Circuit has acknowledged that the copying of a title may have some limited significance of the factors in establishing a copyright infringement claim.[58]

As we discuss in chapter 6, "Copyright Fundamentals," a title alone cannot be copyrighted. The courts invariably find that titles are too general, too abstract to be given copyright protection. But if your title has been copied, that could contribute toward establishing whether the substance of your work has been copied. For example, did the filmmakers copy elements from your script and then find that the title fit so well that they copied that too? That's (probably) infringement. Or did they simply like (and copy) your title and then independently develop a story riffing off the title? That would not be infringement.

At any rate, your title should be taken into account if the same title is applied to another's work that (allegedly) copies yours.

INTRINSIC TEST: TOTAL CONCEPT AND FEEL

The intrinsic test really is not much of a test at all. Instead, it's a subjective judgment as to whether two works are or are not similar.[59]

Unlike the extrinsic test (which isolates and analyzes numerous elements individually), the intrinsic test looks broadly at the "total concept and feel" of the two works. This analysis is done by a jury, without the assistance of any experts, and asks "whether the ordinary, reasonable audience would recognize the [filmmaker's] work as a 'dramatization' or 'picturization' of the [aggrieved spec writer's] work."[60]

If you can get past the experts and the judge on the extrinsic test, given its vigorous analysis, convincing a jury using the total-concept-and-feel mode of the intrinsic test should be relatively easy. It seems that people are quick to see similarities and tend to focus on those even in the face of significant differences.

And that's why most copyright infringement cases will never reach a jury. Shrewd studio defendants will likely settle the case in the unlikely event the plaintiff makes it past the extrinsic test on summary judgment.

INVERSE RATIO RULE

Taken together, access and substantial similarity are the circumstantial way of establishing copying. That is,

Access + Substantial Similarity = Copying

But what's the relative weight between access and substantial similarity in this equation? In the extreme case of striking similarity, even if you have no evidence of access whatsoever, you might still prevail if—only if—the similarity between your spec and their film is not just substantial but actually rises to the level of striking.

But what if you do have a very strong showing of access? A high degree of access allows for a lower standard of proof to show substantial similarity.[61] This is known as the inverse ratio rule:

Access ↑ + Substantial Similarity ↓ = Copying

You still have to show substantial similarity, but less proof is needed.

Fortunately for writers, the equation only works one way. That is, no case has ever held that a weak showing of access forces you to make a higher showing of substantial similarity.

Remember, access is only part of the equation. Access does not equal copying. No amount of access is sufficient to show copying if there are no similarities.[62]

Ultimately, it all comes down to substantial similarity. That's where the true fight is.

SUBSTANTIAL SIMILARITY REDUX

Is your head spinning after the last dozen pages? At the risk of oversimplifying, perhaps we can help clarify with a recap.

The Ninth Circuit's two-prong test for substantial similarity can be summarized as follows:

Extrinsic/ Judge	*Intrinsic/ Jury*
Isolating and analyzing individual elements	Total-concept-and-feel comparison
Separate elements	Work as a whole
Judge decides	Jury decides
On pre-trial motion or at trial	At trial only

| Expert witness opinions allowed to assist the judge | No expert opinions allowed to assist the jury |

The extrinsic test comes first, is much more analytically vigorous, and tends to favor filmmakers. Indeed, the decisions in Ninth Circuit cases over the last twenty-five years have overwhelmingly been in favor of filmmakers and against aggrieved writers.

But if you can get past the first prong and get your claim in front of a jury, the intrinsic test is much more favorable to aggrieved writers.

SUMMARY DIAGRAM: COPYRIGHT INFRINGEMENT IN A NUTSHELL

We want to share with you an elegant mnemonic for copyright infringement. It's a simple diagram that not only captures the prima facie elements of copyright infringement, but also reflects the order of analysis.

We start with the copyright symbol itself:

This is such a universally recognized symbol that it's impossible to forget. So much so, that we half expect it to appear as a clue in a Dan Brown thriller. And, in fact, there is a bit of the Dan Brown symbol-as-code to this.

The copyright symbol can be reduced to its component parts, an "O" circling a "C":

"O" and "C" are the initials for the two elements of a copyright infringement prima facie case.

"O" is for ownership. Only a copyright owner has the right (i.e., standing) to bring an infringement action. Ownership is presumed by holding a valid registration.

"C" is for copying. Of course, you never get direct evidence of copying; copying is shown circumstantially by demonstrating access and substantial similarity:

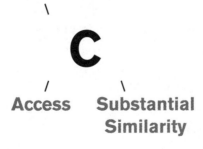

As we all know, access is never the main or controlling issue. Indeed, often the filmmakers concede access and move on to the real fight—substantial similarity.

The two tests for substantial similarity have the abbreviations that appear at the start of all slug lines in a screenplay— EXT. and INT.

\
Substantial Similarity
/ \
EXT. INT.

EXT. means extrinsic in an infringement case and "exterior" in a screenplay. Both suggest something outside.

For the extrinsic analysis, the judge pulls the various elements out of the film and analyzes them separately. It's an objective test, examining story elements, usually with the assistance of expert witnesses. (Of course, the extrinsic analysis is limited to copyrightable portions of the subject work and does not include those elements that were, in effect, not owned by the plaintiff in the first place, e.g., *scènes à faire* and anything from the public domain.)

If the plaintiff gets past the EXT. test, then he gets to the jury for the INT. INT. means intrinsic in an infringement case and "interior" in a screenplay. Both suggest something inside.

For the intrinsic analysis, the jury alone reviews the works. This is a subjective test in which the jury compares the overall look and feel of the works.

The full picture, copyright infringement in a nutshell:

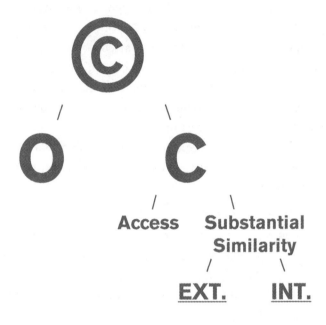

WHAT WILL THE OTHER SIDE ARGUE?

Up until now, in discussing whether you have a "good case" for copyright infringement, we have focused only on *your* allegations; in particular, on whether you have enough of the required elements to state a valid claim, and if so, the likely strength of your case.

But strength is somewhat relative. To get a more realistic picture of the strength of your case, you must anticipate what the other side will say and argue in response to your claim.

What's their factual position? What's their legal defense?

To anticipate what the other side might contend, let's look at the possible and likely defenses and affirmative defenses. What's the difference between a defense and an affirmative defense? And does it matter to you?

The distinction is somewhat technical, but it is important. Indeed, it can become critical because that distinction determines who—you or the alleged infringers—has the burden of proving certain facts.

A defense goes to *negate* part of your claim. For example, you say the production company had *access* to your spec because

1. you sent a query letter to the production company,

2. you received an email response from the production company asking you to send your spec to them, and

3. you did in fact send your spec to the production company, about two years before the infringing film was released.

But the production company—amazingly—says it never saw your spec. Who has the burden of proof?

Because the element of *access* is required for a copyright infringement claim, and you're the one making the claim, you have the burden of proving *access*. You must establish the facts in 1, 2, and 3, above.

An affirmative defense *goes beyond* your claim. Even if you establish all the elements of your claim, the other side may establish *additional* facts that exonerate them. An affirmative defense, as the name implies, affirms an additional element beyond your prima facie case and excuses the copyright infringement or breach of contract.[63]

To continue the example, say the production company claims that

4. when you sent the spec script to them—*which they still maintain they did not actually read*—you also signed and returned the production company's release and waiver form, according to which you have waived the right to sue them for copyright infringement, and

5. the supposedly infringing film was already in pre-production with a final shooting script prior to your sending your spec to them.

Your claim alleged certain facts (numbers 1–3), and in its defense, the production company alleges additional facts (numbers 4 and 5), facts that go beyond your claim and try to set up affirmative defenses. The production company must establish facts 4 and 5.

Let's examine the common and likely defenses and affirmative defenses to your claims.

1. Denial (Factual): Not True!

You probably learned this defense as a kid on the playground, or maybe from watching 1940s mobster movies. The first line of defense is *denial:* I didn't do it! You claim I did, but it's not true!

In litigation, that translates to factual denial. The other side claims that the "facts" you've alleged in support of your prima facie case are not true and you cannot prove them.

Attacking the facts is rather easy (at least at the pleading stage) and quite typical.

Factual disputes have to be resolved in some type of evidentiary hearing. The evidentiary hearing can occur before trial, with a summary judgment motion hearing based on sworn affidavits from witnesses. Or it can be the trial itself, with witnesses on the stand. Such hearings or a trial occur late in the case, after the parties have had an opportunity to interview each other's witnesses and investigate the facts further.

Typically, your opponents deny that they copied from your script because of

1. *Parallel development:* they developed their project in parallel with yours, without ever knowing that yours existed, or

2. *Independent joint source:* they copied from someone else, not from you.

There are a number of defenses that are based on a denial of your alleged facts.

PARALLEL DEVELOPMENT

Parallel development is a hybrid of factual denial.

The production company denies using your material and goes on to explain the existence of its project as a result of "parallel development." Parallel development sounds a lot like "zero access" but is not necessarily the same. The production company may have had some access, maybe even significant access. But if your material was not actually used in developing its project, then there was no copying. No copying means no infringement.

How can you try to prove that they used your material in developing theirs? By comparing the two projects for substantial similarity.

INDEPENDENT JOINT SOURCE

Independent joint source is another hybrid of factual denial. The production company denies copying from you and instead claims that it actually copied from someone else.

Was the common idea behind both projects just in the air, a function of the cultural zeitgeist? Or are both projects traceable to a common source?

If the common source is in the public domain, then the parallel development is permissible. (See the section on *Amistad* in chapter 9, "Confessions of an Expert Witness.")

If the third-party common source is protected intellectual property, then both secondary users are infringers.

Now let's talk about another type of denial.

2. Denial (Legal): True, but So What?

As discussed above, factual denial is where the other side challenges you to come forward and prove your facts as true. Factual denial says, "Not true!"

In sharp contrast, legal denial assumes that your facts are indeed all true, but the other side argues that those facts nevertheless aren't enough to state a claim as a matter of law. Legal denial says, "True, but so what? So what if I did as you claim? Nothin' wrong with that!"

If legal denial is going to come up, it will come up right at the beginning of a case, during the pleading phase.

The other side is basically saying that there's a flaw in your legal position; that even if your factual allegations are taken as the gospel truth, they are still insufficient to state a claim because

- you've omitted a required factual allegation, or
- you're wrong in your interpretation of the law as applied to your facts.

Defending your legal position is somewhat complicated and nuanced and will require that your counsel file a research brief with the court for determination. Unfortunately— or perhaps fortunately—your role at this point will be to sit back and *let your lawyer carry the argument.*

3. *Wrong Court: State versus Federal Court*

Not all courts can hear all types of lawsuits. Are you in the right court for your case?

The answer to that question turns on the type of lawsuit you're bringing. The Copyright Act is a federal statute. Only a federal court can hear copyright disputes.[64] So if your claim is that someone has infringed on your copyrighted work, or you want the court to determine and declare who legally holds a copyright in a particular work, then you must take your case to federal court.

There is no state copyright law.[65] And state courts are not authorized to hear copyright disputes.[66] So a writer would never bring a claim in state court, right? Wrong.

Not all claims are copyright claims. You will recall from our discussion in chapter 4, "Selling to Others," that idea theft claims are contract claims, not copyright claims.

Breach of contract and implied contract are creations of state law.[67] These are your classic idea theft cases.

But what if you have *both* idea theft and copyright infringement claims?[68]

Since only federal courts can hear federal copyright cases, a mixed copyright/contract case could only be heard in federal court. Remember, a state court can *never* hear a federal copyright claim. A federal court *can* hear your state contract claim along with the copyright infringement claim.

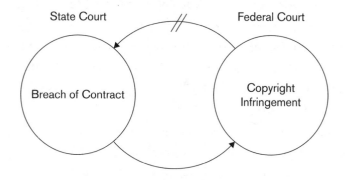

NO SUBJECT MATTER JURISDICTION

Why does court selection matter? After all, if you happen to choose the wrong court initially, can't you just refile in the proper court?

Not necessarily. For a while, producers used a defense strategy based on subject matter jurisdiction to get cases dismissed on venue technicalities.

Here's how the trick/trap works:

    1. You file your complaint in state court. You might not even claim under a copyright theory (because you and/or your attorney know better!). Your claim

is for breach of implied contract, a classic idea theft claim. You allege that you pitched the producers in their office on the lot and left behind a two-pager of your story.

2. The producers argue to the state court that your claim is really just a copyright claim in disguise, putting heavy emphasis on your short treatment, which after all is "an original work of authorship fixed in [a] tangible medium of expression."[69] They argue that your case really should be in federal court.

3. The wise and/or overworked superior court judge agrees, dismissing your case (thereby reducing the superior court's caseload), and suggests that you refile in federal court.

4. So you refile in federal court.

5. Now the producers argue to the federal court that there is insufficient original work product in your short treatment (a mere two-pager) for copyright protection. That is, your treatment consists of stock characters, general themes, *scènes à faire* structure, and otherwise unprotectable material. (Of course it does—it's a two-pager! Nothing could be fleshed out or developed in that small a space!) But you maintain that your two-page treatment gave them the idea for "their" film. The producers emphasize to the court that mere ideas cannot be copyrighted.

6. The court agrees and dismisses your case.

7. There's nowhere left to take your claim. You're out of state court. You're out of federal court. You're out of luck.

How could you have avoided this trap? What could you and/or your attorney have done differently? There are two possible strategies.

First, you could show that you have a "plus factor" that allows you to stay in state court—something beyond a mere non-infringement promise, because a promise not to infringe is effectively the same protection against infringement that you already have under the Copyright Act.

Second, you could show a sufficient basis to maintain a copyright claim and therefore stay in federal court. Because once the federal court dismisses the copyright claim, it is under no obligation to consider the state court claims. And, of course, you cannot return to state court because the state court closed its doors to you when it dismissed your claims and directed you to federal court.

4. *Statute of Limitations: Too Late, Time's Up*

Nothing ratchets up dramatic tension like a ticking clock.

Litigation has its own ticking clock—the deadline to bring a lawsuit is called the statute of limitations. You've probably heard this term before, as in "There's no statute of limitations for murder" and "Keep your tax records at least until the statute of limitations runs out."

As the name implies, a statute of limitations is the law that limits the amount of time within which you can file a lawsuit. When you see a film that appears to have been stolen from your spec script, many things will be racing through your mind. But the deadline to sue will probably not be one of them.

Timing can be everything.

Attorneys (and their malpractice insurance carriers) obsess over deadlines. Once the case filing deadline passes, your rights pass as well. So even if you could have won your case hands down on the merits, you now lose because the deadline has passed. Yes, you read that right.

So how much time do you have? Naturally, if your work has been infringed upon, you're going to want to act as quickly as possible. Indeed, you're probably boiling mad and can't help but act fast. You want justice and you want it now.

But the process slows you down. You hunt for a lawyer. You interview a number of potential lawyers. You tell your story, again and again. You ask each prospective lawyer about your chances. You find a lawyer you like—or perhaps more importantly, one who likes you. You discuss strategy. You discuss costs. But all this time, the clock is ticking.

How much time do you have?

The length of the statute of limitations depends upon the type of claim that you're bringing:

two years for breach of implied contract/oral
    contract;[70]
three years for copyright infringement;[71] and
four years for breach of written contract.[72]

So the statute of limitations tells you the deadline when the clock *stops* ticking. But when does the clock *start* ticking?

Let's suppose:

A production company makes a film based on your
    spec script without your permission— indeed,

completely without your knowledge. The film has limited theatrical release in Los Angeles only. In fact, it plays only a couple of days on one screen at the Laemmle Five on Sunset Boulevard. After that it goes to DVD or streaming video.

You never see or even hear about this film. (It must have been released during that month of self-exile when you were rewriting your next spec.)

Is the clock ticking for you yet?

The copyright statute of limitations starts to run when:

1. You actually learn about the infringement. That is, you actually see the film yourself; *or*
2. You reasonably should have learned about the infringement. That is,
   a. someone tells you enough about the film to lead you to believe that there might be a possibility of infringement and you should investigate further, *or*
   b. the film is in such wide theatrical release that you reasonably should be aware that it's out there and what it's about, and therefore should investigate further.[73]

Whichever happens first (the date you learn, or the date you should have learned) is when the statute of limitations starts ticking.

If you think you've been wronged, you should act fast. Do your due diligence. Find a lawyer. Get your lawyer's opinion about when the statute of limitations started and when it ends. Otherwise, you really won't know how much time you have.

Then make your decision to sue or not to sue. Otherwise the clock will make the decision for you.

5. Estoppel: Don't Sell Fiction as Fact

Estoppel, translated literally, means *stopping*. As a legal concept and legal phrase of art, it means that you are stopped from bringing a claim *because of your own prior words or conduct*.

In a copyright infringement context, the infringers could claim that they have somehow detrimentally relied on an affirmative representation you made that has now turned out to be false. For example:

1. Let's say that you used to work in a police crime lab, and you have written a collection of short stories that take place in a police crime lab.

2. You take your unpublished book of stories to a pitch meeting. You tell the producer that these are "real-life true stories" taken directly from your experiences. You pitch a few of the stories. The room is flat. You pitch a few more. The room has grown cold.

3. You emphasize to the development executives that these are true stories from your own stint in the police crime lab. *They're authentic, they're real.* The room starts to warm up. You pitch a few more. They ask for your unpublished book as a leave-behind for further consideration.

4. A few weeks later, you get a pass. That is, they pass on you.

5. But the producers then actually use your stories to develop a television series. And they readily admit it. Why?

As you will recall (from chapter 1, "Free for the Taking"), no one owns facts or events. You may have thought that offering up these stories as true gave them added cachet for the potential buyer and for attracting an audience. But in actuality, it made the stories fair game for the slick producers to use because they thought that they were facts in the public domain.[74] They've relied on your affirmative statements that the stories were "real-life true stories."

6. *Release: Permission to Steal*

Remember that boilerplate release form you signed at the request of that production company before you sent your spec to them? You might not have thought much about it at the time because you were anxious or excited to get your spec read. But now would be a good time to go back and see what it really says.

As we discussed earlier (chapter 4, "Selling to Others"), no court in the land has ever invalidated a one-sided, producer-friendly release. Never.

It doesn't matter that you didn't negotiate the terms. No one held a gun to your head and forced you to sign. You may have given your express written and signed consent to theft.

That release form is probably enforceable against you.

7. Statute of Frauds: Are Your Rights to Source Material Granted in Writing?

The statute of frauds is known as the "writing requirement." That is, any transfer of intellectual property must be in writing to be enforceable.

How could that impact your case?

As you may recall (from chapter 2, "Clearance Required"), if your spec uses someone else's intellectual property for source material—such as an underlying short story—then you need authorization to do so. And that authorization must be in writing.[75] Otherwise, you yourself are an infringer, violating the copyright of your source material.

An infringer cannot bring a valid claim for infringement. Remember, part of the prima facie case for a copyright infringement claim is that you are actually the legal copyright owner.[76]

And that segues into the next affirmative defense.

8. License

Did someone else get rights to your source material?

Closely related to the problem of your not having a third-party clearance in writing is the fact that your alleged infringer may have gone out and obtained a transfer of rights to the third-party material that you used as your source. And if that material is not in the public domain (e.g., does not involve factual events from news or history), then you are the infringer. And infringers cannot claim copyright infringement.[77]

CHAPTER SIX

Your Legal Team

As we recommended in chapter 5, "Copyright Infringement," it's best to avoid litigation if you can. Litigation is very expensive, and the deck is stacked against the unknown writer. But if you find yourself embroiled in litigation, or if you're just thinking about disregarding our earlier advice, then this chapter will be helpful.

Here we'll discuss the roles and responsibilities of the three indispensable participants on your litigation team: your lawyer, your expert witness, and you, as client and litigant.

YOUR LAWYER

Inside many a practicing lawyer there's a novelist struggling to be born. The converse is also true: Novelists sometimes yearn to be lawyers. All things considered, it's best if all concerned stick with their own callings.

Hon. Alex Kozinski, Chief Justice, Ninth Circuit Court of Appeals[1]

You *need* a lawyer. The casebooks are filled with examples of writers who tried to go it alone, without an attorney, and lost.[2] In fact, we have yet to see a published case where a writer without an attorney won.

So what does a lawyer bring to the table that you don't already have? Legal expertise and objectivity.

You probably have some level of legal knowledge already. (Of course you do, you're reading this book!) Indeed, you may even be a lawyer yourself. (A number of Writers Guild members are.) But, as the old adage goes, the lawyer representing himself has a fool for a client. Why? The issue is objectivity.

Your lawyer will bring objectivity to your case. You're probably so hopping mad that you're ready to go all the way to the Supreme Court. But if you can't find a competent lawyer who is willing to take your case, it probably means that you don't have a good case. Which is to say, you might not have a basis to win, or the cost-benefit of suing might be so stacked against you, for whatever reason, that even if you win the lawsuit, it is still a net loss for you. More about that later. Let's talk about lawyers.

It's easy to find an attorney; they're everywhere. But it's difficult to find the right attorney.

There are three things that make an attorney right for you: sufficient legal expertise, reputation, and a fee arrangement that you can afford.

Legal Expertise

There are certain lawyering skills that your attorney must have to zealously represent you in your dispute. And you want your attorney to have developed these skills well *before* they met you. It probably is not to your advantage to have your attorney learn these skills for the first time during your case and, in all ways, at your expense. These are the things you need your attorney to know:

Trial work: How many cases have they tried? How many of those were jury trials?

Intellectual property law: Are they well versed in copyright law, and in the law of implied contract and idea theft?

The entertainment milieu: Are they familiar with the players, the studios, the town?

So how do you find the right attorney? Through referrals, and further research based on those referrals.

Referrals from people you know Other writers. Former film school instructors. Your manager or agent. Other lawyers (lawyers who don't specialize in entertainment law but know someone who does). This is an excellent way to find a lawyer.

Referral from bar associations The membership list from the Beverly Hills Bar Association, or other such associations that have an intellectual property or entertainment law practice section. Check out www.bhba.org. This is a good way to find a lawyer.

Referrals from online services Yes, we suppose, but only as a last resort, and with this warning: attorney rating web pages often are full of strangers talking about strangers. That's double strange. On their face, it is very difficult if not impossible to know whether the ratings are based on a valid survey or reliable reporting pool. This is a questionable way to find a lawyer. Unlike client surveys for doctors, where every patient should go away happy and with remedies, with trial lawyers, half the clients will go away losers. So you should question the validity of the survey.

Reputation

You want an attorney who is known favorably in the relevant legal circles. A good reputation means credibility. Credibility is very important.

Credibility means that the judge and the other side take your attorney seriously. And that means, by proxy, that they take you and your case seriously. That makes you a threat. Someone who must be dealt with. Someone who cannot be ignored.

Although an unknown attorney can gain credibility in a particular case as time goes on—by showing competence and reliability—it is a strategic advantage for you to have an attorney who has credibility from the outset.

Attorney's Fees

There are three central models for attorney's fees: contingency, billable hours, and flat fee.

There are also hybrids created by blending these three models. For example, you might have a different fee arrangement for different phases of the lawsuit. Perhaps you'll pay a flat fee for the opening demand letter, and then if you decide to move forward with a lawsuit, an hourly rate or contingency from that point onward. But let's discuss the three models in their most common forms.

CONTINGENCY FEES

A contingency fee arrangement is the most common and customary model for aggrieved writers in copyright infringement cases. As an entertainment professional you're no stranger to contingency compensation. The guilds call it "deferral." In a contingency case, attorneys basically defer their fees until later, contingent upon there being some recovery (after settlement or trial).

If your attorney takes the case "on contingency," then you owe no legal fees during the case. When the case is over, if you have won and recover money, then your attorney gets a percentage of the recovery. One-third (33.3 percent) is most typical. Sometimes there's a sliding scale tied to the point in time when recovery occurs, for example, 25 percent if there's a settlement after only a demand letter, 33.3 percent after that, and 50 percent if the case goes to trial.

There are two advantages to the contingency model. Most obviously, you don't owe any attorney's fees unless you prevail. Further, you and your attorney are both pushing for the same outcome—victory. Neither of you will see any money unless you win.

One subtle disadvantage is that you and your attorney may not be aligned when it comes to evaluating settlement offers. For example, it may be cost effective for your attorney to take a quick settlement up front (i.e., a bird in the hand), whereas you want to go the distance (two birds in the bush) because for you, it's not all about money. And maybe it's not about money at all.

A good example of this tension is found in the film *A Civil Action* (1998).[3] The slick personal injury attorney Jan Schlichtmann, played by John Travolta, wants a fast settlement to achieve a payday, whereas the aggrieved parents he represents want justice for their deceased children and the remaining family. The goals of the attorney and client are not aligned.

This tension—money (contingency attorney) versus justice (contingency client)—makes for good drama on the screen but isn't so good in real life. If it's not about the money—or not *just* about money—for you as a litigant, then you should be careful to find an attorney for whom it's not just about the money either.

A word of warning: contingency is *not* free. Even though your attorney's fees are on contingency, you probably will still need to put hard dollars into your case as it goes forward. There are other routine fees, costs, and expenses of litigation, including:

·   court filing fees;
·   mail and messenger costs;
·   document copying expenses;
·   court reporter fees and expenses for depositions; and
·   expert witness fees (which are significant).

All of these costs and expenses are due up front and are beyond the control of your attorney. Someone will have to pay them when they're due, either you (most likely) or your attorney (much less likely).

A Civil Action serves as a cautionary tale for attorneys. There, a (winnable) environmental toxic tort case taken on contingency bankrupts the law firm because it is carrying all the costs and expenses of the class action lawsuit.

Some attorneys are willing to gamble with their time and take a case on contingency. But they're not willing to gamble with hard cash by advancing fees, costs, and expenses on a contingency case. They'll look to you—the client—to cover those. Even when lawyers agree to front some of the money, they off-set those advances against any recovery and recoup them at the end of the case.

BILLABLE HOURS

In the billable hours model, attorneys charge you for their time. The charge is based on two multipliers: hourly rate and minimum billable increment.

The concept of hourly rate is straightforward; it is the amount an attorney charges for an hour of their time. The hourly rate is often the only number that would-be clients focus on when selecting or retaining counsel.

But the minimum billable increment can be equally important, if not more important. Typically, attorneys charge in increments of a quarter hour (fifteen minutes), a sixth of an hour (ten minutes), or a tenth of an hour (six minutes).

Let's say your attorney's rate is $300 per hour. If you call and talk with the attorney for five minutes, the amount you're billed will depend on the minimum billable increment:

a quarter hour would be $75 ($300 × 0.25),
a sixth of an hour would be $50 ($300 × 0.167), and
a tenth of an hour would be $30 ($300 × 0.10).

As you can see, the smaller the minimum billable increment, the less expensive it is for the client.

FLAT-FEE MODEL

This is the pre-set rate chart billing model. The attorney will take your case for a certain pre-set amount. Your entire obligation for fees is that amount, no matter how much time—or how little time—the case actually takes.

The pre-set rate may be a one-time total due on retention, for example, $250,000, or it may be spread over a series of payments incurred and due in certain phases of the case, such as $25,000 for the pleading phase, another $125,000 through close of discovery and pre-trial, and another $200,000 for trial.

An advantage to the flat-fee method is predictability. You know with absolute certainty the amount of legal fees that you're going to have to pay.

A disadvantage is that it can create a subtle conflict between your attorney and you. You both want to win. You don't care how many hours your attorney has to spend to do so, but your attorney (potentially, at some level, consciously or subconsciously) does. Putting it bluntly, for your attorney, the more time spent, the less money earned. If the flat fee is $250,000 and the attorney spends a hundred hours, that's a reasonable market rate of $250 per hour. But if the case spins out of control and it takes the attorney a thousand hours, that's $25 per hour. Your attorney would make more per hour as an adjunct instructor teaching contracts to paralegals in a community college evening class. You get the picture; you see the inherent tension. The longer the case takes, the more your attorney may come to resent you and/or the case.

An effective hybrid of the flat-fee model is the limited engagement model. As the name implies, you and your attorney agree that the attorney will work on the case for a prescribed and finite time only or for some limited activity. Clients sometimes can't afford a full lawsuit but want to test the waters with their claim. So they'll retain an attorney for the limited purpose of writing and sending a demand letter to the infringers, and perhaps for any early settlement negotiations that immediately result from the demand letter. But that's it. After that, they're on their own unless they sign on for further representation, by that attorney or someone else.

YOUR EXPERT WITNESS

To be a judge is to be a generalist. Judges hear all types of cases, from medical malpractice, to wrongful termination of employment, to insurance coverage disputes, to securities fraud, and beyond. And, yes, upon occasion, copyright infringement and idea theft actions.

Perhaps your judge presided over a copyright infringement/idea theft case before. But that does not make your judge an expert. The judge graduated from law school, not film school. Despite this lack of expertise in the arena of film and television, it is the judge alone who hears and decides the very critical initial part of the two-prong test for substantial similarity.

How does the judge, as a generalist, make an informed decision in the specialized area of substantial similarity of literary works?

The parties educate the judge by using expert witnesses. Your expert witness is more important than your lawyer. Your lawyer is the director, but your expert witness is the on-stage talent.

Expert Witness Testimony and Opinions

Remember the film *My Cousin Vinny*? Brooklyn lawyer Vinny Gambini (played by Joe Pesci), in his first trial ever, is ineptly trying to defend his cousin against first-degree murder charges in a rural Alabama court. It is not the lawyer alone who wins the case. The case is won by the lawyer in concert with the expert witness (Mona Lisa Vito, played by Marisa Tomei).[4] The expert witness turns the case around when she opines that the cousin's car, with its independent suspension, could not possibly have made the type of skid marks found at the scene of the crime.

An expert witness may be used if the expert has *specialized knowledge* that would be helpful in deciding the case correctly, and if the expert's testimony is *sufficiently reliable* to assist the judge and/or jury. Rule 702 of the *Federal Rules of Evidence* is the basic rule concerning the use expert witnesses. Rule 702 states that a witness who is "qualified as an expert by knowledge, skill, experience, training, or education, may testify thereto in the form of an opinion or otherwise" if:

1. the expert's scientific, technical, or other specialized knowledge will assist the trier of fact to understand the evidence or to determine a fact in issue;
2. the testimony is based on sufficient facts or data;

3. the testimony is the product of reliable principles
   and methods; and

4. the expert has reliably applied the principles and
   methods to the facts of the case.

The key is that the expert witness must truly be an
expert in an area of specialized knowledge that is not in
the possession of the judge or jury.
Who qualifies as an expert? There are no rigid requirements. You certainly want your expert to have "blue chip"
credentials, or at least more impressive credentials than the
other side's expert witness. At the very least, "[T]here must
be some indication that [your expert witness] has, in one
capacity or another, watched, read, written, compared,
and/or analyzed literary works."[5]
Expert witness testimony and opinions in copyright
infringement/idea theft cases typically address two issues:

· Protectability: What is protectable? That is, what
  portion of your script should be disregarded as
  scènes à faire or public domain for purposes of a
  substantial similarity comparison?

· Similarity: How do the protectable portions of
  your script compare on an element-by-element or
  side-by-side analysis with the allegedly infringing
  work (i.e., the alleged infringer's shooting script
  and/or film)?

You need an expert witness to testify and render an opinion in these two areas.
Ultimately, to have any hope of winning, your expert
must conclude that significant portions of your script are

protectable, and those portions are substantially similar to the allegedly infringing work. Expert witness testimony is judged just like any other testimony. The judge or jury may accept or reject it. If it is accepted, the judge or jury may give it as much—or as little—weight as they think it deserves, considering the witness's education and experience, the reasons given for the opinion, and all the other evidence in the case.[6]

You need an expert witness (1) to persuade the judge and jury, who are not experts themselves (and worse, might fancy themselves experts simply because they're film buffs), and (2) because the opposing side most certainly will have its own expert testifying in its favor and contrary and to your position.

Working with Your Expert Witness

Your lawyer will find and hire the expert witness on your behalf. You will never have any direct contact with your expert witness. Although communications between you and your attorney are privileged and confidential, communications between you and your expert witness are not.

That means that your expert witness could be compelled to testify regarding any statements you've made to them, including statements that might be harmful to your case. And in the hands of shrewd opposing counsel, most any statement you've made could be construed to cast doubt on your position. Accordingly, your attorney and your expert witness will not open the door to that possibility. You will never have any direct contact with your expert witness.

Since your expert cannot talk with you directly, how will they learn and understand your side of the story? They'll read your complaint, your discovery responses, and your deposition transcript.

Expert Witness Fees

Experts don't work on contingency. They can't. If their fees are contingent on a favorable outcome of your case, then they have a very direct bias. And if they're biased in your favor, that neutralizes their objectivity as an expert witness.

An expert's opinion is supposed to be objective, even if you are paying for it.

If you're paying in advance, the expert is free to say whatever they truly believe and their compensation will not be effected. In addition, just because you've retained an expert witness for an opinion of the case does not mean that you're obligated to use the expert at trial. Indeed, if the expert's opinion were not helpful to your case, your attorney would likely treat the expert as a consultant only and not call them as a witness at trial. The opinion of any consultant who is not designated as an expert witness for trial remains protected from disclosure to the opposing side as attorney-client work product.[7]

Experts Know Best (So You and Your Attorney Need to Listen)

As a potential expert witness, Howard has turned down half (!) of the cases offered to him.

There are many he doesn't remember, largely because he exited early on, and partly because there was no point in remembering them. But his passing on these cases had nothing to do with money. Indeed, he had to take a deep breath in the *Da Vinci Code* case, since he knew it would be a biggie financially.

It's all about honesty, and that translates to credibility.

Howard seldom mentions it, but so far he's not been on the losing side of a copyright case. Not ever. He attributes this absolute success rate not to his importance to the cases, but to the fact that he turns down half of the cases people bring to him because he can't agree with the side that wants to hire him. That's cost him a lot of income and assured that some entertainment attorneys go elsewhere for an expert witness in the future. But it preserves his credibility as an expert witness when he does appear at trial. And ultimately, that's everything.

So if your attorney is having difficulty finding an expert witness, you should ask your attorney why. Is it the fees? Is it the scheduling? Or is it something deeper? Your attorney has an absolute duty of candor to tell you what the problem is.

If potential expert witnesses are rejecting your case on the merits, it is highly likely that a judge and jury would do so also. Find out.

Helpful? Maybe. Necessary? Never

Some opinions cast doubt on whether expert testimony regarding substantial similarity is ever *helpful* when comparing two literary works aimed at a general audience.[8] But the law is clear: expert testimony is never *necessary*.

Although expert witnesses have traditionally been used in copyright infringement cases, especially in the Ninth Circuit (California),[9] there nevertheless is no absolute right to having an expert witness.

Remember, the expert may be yours, but the reason the expert is there is to assist the court. And if the judge does not believe that assistance is needed to determine whether there is substantial similarity, then experts will not be allowed.

The use of expert witness testimony is completely within the discretion of the trial court.[10]

Expert Witness Identity and Opinion Disclosures

Each party must disclose to the other parties the identity of any expert witness it may use at trial.[11] This disclosure must be accompanied by a written report[12]—prepared and signed by the expert witness—that contains:

1. Opinions.   A complete statement of all opinions the expert witness will express and the basis and reasons for them;
2. Evidence considered.   The facts or data considered by the expert witness in forming those opinions; typically, the expert witness will have reviewed all discovery requests and responses, as well as all witness deposition transcripts;
3. Trial exhibits.   Any exhibits that will be used to summarize or support the opinions;
4. Résumé.   The expert witness's qualifications, including a list of all publications authored in the previous ten years;

5. Prior testimony. A list of all other cases in which, during the previous four years, the witness testified as an expert at trial or by deposition; and

6. Fee. A statement of the compensation to be paid for the study and testimony in the case.

After the expert witness written reports are exchanged by the parties, the opposing party or parties will depose your expert witness. And your lawyer will depose the other side's expert witness(es).[13]

As you may know, a deposition is an oral examination—questions and answers—conducted under oath and for use at trail. The central purpose of the expert witness deposition is to lock in the expert's opinion and the basis for the opinion. During the deposition, the other side will go through each and every element in the expert witness report, as well as any assumptions or information that your attorney provided and that your expert relied on.[14]

The expert witness deposition will be exhaustive—and likely exhausting—but it does have an inherent limitation. The other side is required to pay for your expert's time spent in the deposition.[15] And, unfortunately, you will be required to pay for their expert's time when your attorney takes their deposition.

YOU, AS A CLIENT AND A LITIGANT

Not all experts make it to trial. Some experts will turn down your case. Or they'll review the case material, but their opinion is not helpful to your case, and you'll turn them down.

Either way, you should insist that your lawyer make you aware of such experts. These experts are your devil's advocate—they will tell you the weaknesses in your case and what the other side is likely to argue.

Most trial attorneys—strike that—most *litigation* attorneys (the ones who push the paper and typically operate more on hormones than intellect) frequently get too close to their big cases to take the cautionary advice of their first-choice expert. Instead, because these attorneys fancy themselves giant killers—and here we're talking about a famous celebrity giant (the best kind)—they don't want to hear "no" when they've already committed to the client and the case with their own investment of "yes."

Experienced trial attorneys usually retain their expert before committing to the case themselves. This is especially true of copyright cases, since the threshold issue—whether the plaintiff has proffered any protectable literary property—is one for the court with the assistance of expert testimony. If you don't have a solid expert, you don't have a case. So here are your takeaways:

1. As a client/plaintiff/writer, take careful heed whenever a potential expert witness will not take the job and join your team—especially if the witness has the professional courtesy to give a debriefing as to why.

2. Stay engaged with your lawyer and your case to make sure that you are aware whenever an expert declines.

3. Finally, if your expert of choice declines, it might be time for Plan B. Perhaps the case is not as strong

as you or your lawyer think? Perhaps it's time to consider a reasonable settlement rather than a great trial?

These are just more of the many steps in the uphill battle a writer faces in the war of attrition that is copyright infringement/idea theft litigation.

CHAPTER SEVEN

Confessions of an Expert Witness

Free for the Telling

Howard is much too much of a mensch to admit it, much less to ever say it, so I will say it instead: Howard Suber is *the* premier expert consultant and witness in the United States for substantial similarity issues in film and television.

Having regularly lunched together since my graduation from UCLA film school in 2003, we've shared many an entertaining discourse, from literature to litigation. As a lawyer, most of my really interesting entertainment law stories remain confidential under the attorney-client communication privilege, even after the matters have long been resolved. Similarly, many of Howard's expert witnessing matters remain confidential per private non-disclosure agreements he's signed.

But, in this chapter, we wanted to share with you some of Howard's more high-profile matters that are legally free for the telling.

The general public, as well as many lawyers, often think of expert witnesses as hired guns who will say whatever someone pays them to say. It's certainly true that, as a trial attorney, I've *never* called an expert witness to the stand who disagrees with my client's position. But that doesn't mean that our expert is pandering to our position. Rather, it means that I won't use an expert witness who disagrees with our position. And that means I'll keep looking until I find the right expert witness—or perhaps I won't use an expert at all. As mentioned in chapter 6, "Your Legal Team," no one is required to use an expert witness, and some courts may decide that experts are not necessary and disallow their use.

Howard has had debates with other expert witnesses who see what they do as being similar to what lawyers do: namely, advocating for their clients. We disagree. An advocate argues, and arguments are not evidence. But an expert witness testifies, and their expert opinion is evidence.

Expert witnesses are required to tell the truth.[1] That means, of course, the truth as they see it. This doesn't necessarily mean they're correct; it merely means that they won't say things they don't really believe to be true. That is why, over a forty-year span, Howard has turned down more matters than he's accepted. It's also why he's not biased toward a particular side, with the matters that he has accepted being equally split between plaintiffs and defendants. His touchtone has been the truth.

So, in his own words:

COMING TO AMERICA (1988)

Coming to America was the most high-profile idea theft case of the twentieth century. I was the principal expert witness for the plaintiffs.

Journalist Art Buchwald and his producer partner, Alan Bernheim, each signed a contract with Paramount Pictures that contained wording explicitly stating that if the studio used the "original story and concept" from Buchwald and his partner, the two would be entitled to compensation. The two submitted a short treatment to the studio that included these three points:

· Eddie Murphy (then one of the most commercially successful comedians in the entertainment industry) would play an African prince;
· He comes to an American ghetto, where he takes a menial job and enjoys life with his friend; and
· He falls in love.

The treatment was twice optioned by Paramount, but the studio couldn't get a writer to craft an acceptable screenplay. Eventually, the options lapsed, and Buchwald and Bernheim were free to shop the project elsewhere, which they did. Warner then optioned the project and began development but dropped it when they learned the Paramount was shooting a film titled *Coming to America* with Eddie Murphy.

Two years later, in 1988, *Coming to America* came out and was an enormous commercial success. The concept of the film was attributed to Eddie Murphy and the film's costar, Arsenio Hall.

Although sometimes mistakenly referred to as a copyright case, this one was actually about the contract Buchwald and Bernheim had signed with Paramount Studios. As we've pointed out earlier, copyright is determined by federal laws and trials are held in federal courts. Contract law, however, is different from state to state, and contract law cases are tried in state courts. This one was tried in the California State Superior Court in Los Angeles County.[2]

When Paramount refused to acknowledge that Buchwald and Bernheim had made any significant contribution to *Coming to America*, Buchwald and his partner sued for breach of contract. I was asked to analyze the single paragraph Buchwald and Bernheim had submitted and compare it to the finished film. (Eddie Murphy, at that time Paramount's biggest star, and Arsenio Hall were never involved in the lawsuit.)

Arguments about similarities can be difficult to grasp, especially when someone else is arguing that the similarities *aren't* really similar. To avoid a pointless "'Tis too/'Tain't neither" spat, I offered what was in effect testimony from Paramount's own marketing department, in the form of a VHS tape of the movie as released and some copies of Paramount's posters.

In the film industry, the marketing department is responsible for coming up with the "key art" for a film. This is the image, icon, brand or whatever you want to call it that will forever link certain visuals and texts with that specific film. They will be used in trailers, ads, posters, and on the sides of buses and sometimes (at least in Los Angeles and New York) the sides of buildings. They will be on the side of the containers for the DVD or Blu-ray releases of movies. Key art is the image on your television set that you click on to watch a film. Studios and distributors spend an enormous amount of time and money on key art graphics, so they think very carefully about what they are selling.

Here's what was on the posters and VHS tape shown to the judge in the Buchwald case: Eddie Murphy is an African prince in fine robes, gold chains, and a crown. The skyline of New York City is behind him. In the trailers, he takes a menial job at a McDonald's, lives in the ghetto, and falls in love and marries an American woman.

The judge found in favor of Buchwald and Bernheim, and the case became famous.[3]

But the story doesn't end there. The judge awarded $800,000 in damages to the plaintiff and a very modest amount in lawyer's fees. But Buchwald's legal team spent $3 million on fighting the case, and I was told Paramount spent $4 million.

At best, this was a Pyrrhic victory for Buchwald and Bernheim, and the case provides an example of why people who want to sue over a contested film should proceed with extreme caution.

The good news is that this case reinforces the rule that ideas *are* protectable under written or implied-in-fact contracts. The bad news is that the costs of waging a lawsuit against a major Hollywood studio are so high that they make the idea of "victory" in such cases very problematic.

AMISTAD (1997)

When two or more filmmakers base their films on the same or similar source material, concerns about copyright and who owns what are bound to show up. *Dr. Strangelove* (1968) was in production at the same time *Fail-Safe* (1964) was in production. Stanley Kubrick and the producers started a legal battle that ended with Columbia buying the rights to the source material for both films. In other cases, if the two productions can't merge their projects, each side races to get to market first. Usually, the first one there does better at the box office.

In the case of Steven Spielberg's *Amistad*, a writer sued DreamWorks, of which Mr. Spielberg was a partner, claiming the studio and director had stolen her novel about the 1830 case of the infamous *Amistad* slave ship, which a group of enslaved Africans seized control of and landed in North America.[4] She sued Spielberg and his associates shortly before the marketing campaign for the film was set to launch—the most vulnerable time for the distributor because there was now a large investment that needed to be recouped, plus a large amount of advertising money about to be spent. The plaintiff's lawyers asked the court to prevent the film's release, which would, of course, have been disastrous.

In my declaration for the defense, I compared the plaintiff's book with Howard Jones's *Mutiny on the Amistad*, a book published earlier than the plaintiff's and one that DreamWorks had purchased and on which they claimed to have based their movie. I demonstrated that the plaintiff had herself taken whole passages nearly verbatim from Jones's book and incorporated them into her own novel, which she was now claiming DreamWorks had stolen from her.

An article on the comparisons and the lawsuit appeared on the front page of the *New York Times*, and, in an interview with a reporter, the plaintiff said that the material she took from the book DreamWorks owned was historical in nature and was thus free for the taking. My point exactly. Ultimately, the plaintiff withdrew the lawsuit and praised Spielberg's *Amistad* as "a splendid piece of work."

TWISTER (1996)

This case involved another Spielberg film (the more money you make in film, the more likely you are to get sued). A screenwriter living in Missouri was able to have his lawsuit against *Twister* tried in his home state, rather than in Southern California, where most film copyright cases are adjudicated. Studios much prefer to try their cases in courts in their own area and prefer cases decided by judges, not juries. This is because of widespread public belief that everyone from Hollywood lies, cheats, and steals to achieve their goals and then tells whatever lies are necessary to cover up their crimes.

The fact that the case, despite the filmmakers' lawyer's best efforts, was tried in Missouri and before a jury, realized the lawyer's worst fears. It received front-page coverage during a long trial—undoubtedly because the famous writer Michael Crichton was one of the writers and producers and Steven Spielberg was executive producer.

The plaintiff claimed he had invented the idea of doing a film on tornado chasers and, furthermore, that he had invented the idea of mixing a love story with a disaster film. A humongous number of lawyers, not just from the production company, DreamWorks, but also from the insurance company and others with a vested interest, were involved, and a jury consultant was assigned to prep me on how to deal with juries. After months of preparation and multiple meetings, I was scheduled to be the last witness.

For months, the defense lawyers had begged Spielberg to appear, but he refused, considering the case to be so ridiculous that he didn't need to show up. But on the last day of the trial, I was awakened by a defense attorney bearing the news that Spielberg had changed his mind and had just arrived. I was told that he had left the plane's engine running because he was sure the trial wouldn't take long. Thus, I was bumped to make room for Mr. Spielberg's Indiana Jones–like last-minute rescue. Ever the master storyteller, he related to the jury that he had been interested in twisters ever since he was a kid watching the water swirl down his bathtub drain. The jury loved it and found for the defense.

TREASURE PLANET (2002)

I've been hired several times to do what I call "prophylactic consulting" in the area of copyright. This occurs when a production company developing a film or television series asks my advice about the resemblance of their project to a similar one that a competing company has already made or is preparing to make.

In this instance, Twentieth Century-Fox was planning an animated film based on Robert Louis Stevenson's book *Treasure Island*, which the studio released as *Titan A.E.* (2000). Their concern was that the Walt Disney Company was planning its own animated version of Stephenson's novel, to be released as *Treasure Planet* (2002). Fox had two concerns: one of the producers working on Fox's film had previously worked for Disney on its competing project, and Disney had released *Treasure Island* as a live-action film in 1950.

There was no question that Robert Louis Stevenson's 1883 novel was in the public domain. That's why there had been thirteen previous versions filmed—anybody was free to make their own. Disney has for years had the reputation of being the most litigious of the Hollywood studios, quick to sue others for stealing from its properties. This is somewhat ironic, since, beginning with its first feature-length animated film, *Snow White and the Seven Dwarfs* (1937), Disney has been addicted to making films based on the work of others—fifty of its films have been based on works in the public domain. While others have been free to use the same public domain works, Disney has been quite insistent—and legally correct—that others can't base their films on *Disney's* versions of films such as *Pinocchio, Cinderella, Alice in Wonderland, Sleeping Beauty, Robin Hood, Beauty and the Beast,* or *The Jungle Book.*

This position is upheld by the law. Disney is entitled to "steal" any story that is no longer protected by copyright—and so is everybody else ("steal" here being a colloquialism for "use"). But this applies only to the common source material. If you use anything Disney created that was *not* in the original source, Disney is entitled to immediately sue for copyright infringement.

The problem is, where do the elements derived from a common source end and the original material created by Disney begin? It's often a difficult question, which is why other companies tread carefully. Not wanting to be accused of copying Disney's work, either from its 1950 live-action version of *Treasure Island* or through the prior work of the Fox employee who had previously worked at Disney, Fox's attorneys asked me to compare the 1950 film and what they knew about the script and the visuals for Disney's forthcoming film.

Over a long pre-production period, I read early scripts Fox had developed and advised the studio that the first draft had only a few minor potential problems. These could have been easily fixed without substantively changing the nature of the film. But as the drafts kept coming out (penned, as is usual in Hollywood, by different writers hired in sequential order), I thought they had taken a potentially strong story and, over time, weakened it. However, they hadn't hired me to evaluate their creative efforts. I felt *too* much concern for possible copyright infringement had been demonstrated throughout the process, and that they ended far, far way from the original *Treasure Island*, let alone from Disney's product. The film did not do well.

THE DA VINCI CODE (2006)

A novelist wanted to sue fellow novelist Dan Brown and Columbia Studios for stealing his material for the immensely successful book and film *The Da Vinci Code*. A major Los Angeles law firm, convinced it had a sure thing, approached me to testify on behalf of the plaintiff.

Both the book and the film had been enormous commercial successes, and Dan Brown was at the time one of the highest-paid writers on earth, so it clearly would be a major case. But after reading the arguments from both sides, I shocked the law firm by declining to take the case. The plaintiff's lawyers (I always deal with the lawyers, not directly with the plaintiff or defendant) explained in detail why they thought they had a strong case. I responded by pointing out that while the two books indeed shared many similar elements, all of those on which the plaintiff based his claim of copyright infringement were either historical facts or had been made up by him and presented *as if* they were facts.

Court cases have long ruled that if plaintiffs come into court with "dirty hands"—that is, they've done something ethically or legally suspect—they can't then turn around and claim someone who used the same material is guilty of infringement. So if an author presents something he or she has made up as historically factual, the author cannot then claim infringement if someone else believes that (false) claim and presents it as historical fact (which is not copyrightable).

The large Los Angeles firm that had approached me to work with them decided not to represent the would-be plaintiff after all, so the plaintiff continued to look for a law firm that would. As one might predict, he found such a firm, on the opposite side of the country.[5] They lost.

THE EXORCIST (1973)

This was my first job as an expert witness. When *The Exorcist* opened in a San Francisco theater in 1973, an Italian producer saw it as he was shooting part of a low-budget horror film in the city. He went back to work and inserted key special-effects scenes, such as a young girl's head turning 320 degrees, projectile vomiting, levitation of a bed, and so on.

When the studio's lawsuit went to trial, the defense tried to argue that the similarities (which were self-evident to the judge) were merely ideas, and the Italian producer had not copied the *expression* of *The Exorcist*. For example, the defendant's expert claimed that the young girl's head in their film rotated only 280 degrees, not the 320 degrees (or whatever it was) that the young girl's head rotated in *The Exorcist*. Furthermore, they argued, the comedians Laurel and Hardy had a head-turning gag in one of their films, so head-turning was not unique to *The Exorcist*.

I chose not to quibble about the details of the special effects, such as how many degrees of rotation there were, but to deal with the underlying storytelling *function* of each of the effects. For example, I said the function of scenes such as the head-turning and levitation was to demonstrate there was supernatural power at work within the young girl. The defendant lost and was barred from distributing his film in the United States, but he did get it on screens in other countries.[6] Last I heard, he was living in Beverly Hills.

MEDICINE MAN (1992)

Screenwriter Tom Schulman and the Walt Disney Company were sued for copyright infringement in their film *Medicine Man*. The plaintiff claimed that Schulman, who had won an Academy Award for Best Original Screenplay in 1989 for *Dead Poets Society*, had taken key elements from the plaintiff's unpublished script. (This seems to me to be the commonest claim in film copyright cases, and the claim is, I think, most often presented by the writer of a spec script that has not yet been made.)

Schulman dangled in the wind for months after the trade press published reports saying he had been accused of stealing someone else's screenplay. As in all legal actions, although the legal system demands that an accused person is innocent until proven guilty, in real life, accusations like this cast a shadow over a project and its creators, and sometimes people remember the accusation long after the person accused has been cleared.

When I was retained as an expert witness, I found five or six points out of the dozens the plaintiff had listed that I thought really demanded to be analyzed—most were just willy-nilly comparisons or were based on fundamental mis-understandings of copyright law, and I chose not to make the mistake of thinking I had to answer everything. My favorite was the plaintiff's claim that a key discovery in the protagonist's search for a cure for cancer was contained in a substance carried by a yellow plant, and in Schulman's script, the secret sauce was carried by yellow *ants*. The plaintiff's expert witness claimed the fact that both the ants and plants were yellow constituted a smoking gun, and he cited another example: in the opening scene of both screen-plays, the protagonist arrives at a rural airport in South America and the stage directions note that he is a white man in a sea of brown faces. I'd like to tell you such flimsy "similarities" are rare, but I can't lie to you.

This case did not move beyond summary judgment, when the judge ruled against the plaintiff and did not allow the case to go forward to a jury.

BEATLEMANIA

This was not a copyright case but one involving a group of musicians impersonating the Beatles and was an early suit in the 1980s involving what is now called "the right of pub-licity." (Shows called *Beatlemania* continue to this day.)

Owners of music copyrights, unlike owners of such things as books, plays, and films, are subject to what is called a "compulsory license," which mean they are obligated by law to license their music upon payment of royalty fees determined by an impartial committee. This is why there can be dozens of "covers" of the same song performed by a wide variety of artists.

Some theatrical producers created a roadshow production called *Beatlemania*, which they advertised as "So Real You'll Think You're There!" The producers duly paid for compulsory licenses to parts of the Beatles' songbook. However, the producers of the roadshow also wanted to imitate the Beatles' looks, costumes, gestures, and so on, to fulfill the claim that their show would be "just like" the Beatles. Even though the band refused to grant permission, the producers put together touring companies around the world in which four lookalikes dressed up in the familiar costumes of the Beatles, imitated their mannerisms, cut their hair, and did whatever else they could to appear "just like" the Beatles. They took in something like $40 million.

When the Beatles sued, the producers backtracked and claimed their show wasn't about the Beatles after all but was about the 1960s as seen through the music of the Fab Four. As evidence, they pointed to the newsreels of the era that were projected behind the singers.

I was retained by the Beatles' lawyers to explain to the court which elements were key to the public persona of the Beatles. The case was settled out of court, and the Beatles received several million of the dollars the producers had collected. As in this lawsuit, most copyright and other forms of intellectual property cases are settled out of court because both sides tend to be worried about juries, whose conclusions about similarities are often unpredictable.

SIX FEET UNDER (2001–2005)

The plaintiff was an independent film director who had made a film that few people saw. She pointed out that both her film and the HBO series *Six Feet Under* were about two brothers who take over their deceased father's funeral home business, along with other similarities, and claimed that HBO had ripped her off in making the television series. She was, however, highly selective in pointing out similarities between the two projects, neglecting to mention, for example, that the two brothers were *not* the protagonists of her film, but rather a woman who was a psychopathic serial murderer.

Now, it is an established principle of copyright law that an infringer can't escape negative judgment by pointing out what they *didn't* take. But how does a court or a jury determine how material that *isn't* present relates to material that is? Once again, we see how complex copyright is, and why each case can be different.

The plaintiff's expert witness was a well-known speaker and author of books on screenwriting who had apparently been given the template the Ninth Circuit Court of Appeals favors. He provided a step-by-step comparison of tone, pace, and other elements in the two works that are seldom argued in copyright cases. My favorite—which I've never seen before or since—was his claim that the two works included the same *themes,* among them "man's inhumanity to man." My response was so do *Oedipus Rex,* all the tragedies of Shakespeare, and most memorable popular films. As for his claim that they shared the theme "to thine own self be true," I responded, "And what major dramatic work has the theme 'To thine own self be false'?" The court found in favor of HBO.[7]

All too often, plaintiffs in copyright cases think that if they fill page after page with alleged similarities, the sheer volume will convince a court that they've been robbed. But I've never seen it work out like that. High school or college plagiarists may copy long sections of something they've read and try to pass it off as their own. But nobody making a film or television series for mass consumption is stupid enough to copy so much material that it will jump out at a judge or jury by its sheer quantity.

Epilogue

Creativity and Copyright

THE DEATH OF COPYRIGHT?

Our goal in writing this book has been to help writers understand how copyright laws restrain them, but equally, how copyright laws free them to create.

What if there were no copyright laws? Would writers stop writing? Not many, and probably not the best. Creative people create because they have to, because they feel most fulfilled when they are attempting to bring into the world something new.

In any field, those who create because they think it will make them rich and famous are, more often than not, doomed to disappointment. Yes, a small percentage of all creators do become rich and famous, but so do a small percentage of Olympic athletes and people who place their rent money on a gambling table in Las Vegas.

If there were no copyright laws, would you stop writing?

What creative people need to understand is that the laws regarding copyright usually provide very limited benefits to screenwriters. The value copyright makes possible is mostly for the benefit of the producer, studio, distributor, network, or entity that *takes* control of the copyright.

You might think that copyright exists to protect the potential profits of the person who created a given work. That's certainly what most people, including most creative people, think. In the modern world, the economic reality is that copyright law exists to protect the rights of the copyright owner, who is very seldom the writer but is generally a multinational corporation with large assets. That's why at the end of all Hollywood movies there is text that reads, "For purposes of copyright [studio or production company name] is the author of this work."

But let's suppose, for a moment, that there were no intellectual property rights for screenplays, that *everything* were free for the taking. Would the entertainment industry shut down?

Of course not. But where and how would it get its material? What would give one writer a competitive advantage over another? Perhaps it's who you know. Perhaps it's all about relationships.

But isn't it already about relationships? To a considerable extent, yes. And that's true for most every business or institution, not just entertainment. If you have a toothache, you are likely to ask a friend, "Do you know of a good dentist?" Doctors, lawyers, engineers, and other professionals are likely to recommend people they know. We rely on personal relationships because there's often experience behind them. We know what the person has done in the past and we take that as a good indication of what they will do in the future.

Often, what is more important than your copyright in a specific work are the relationships it makes possible, the reputation it gives you for being able to deliver a saleable work, and the proof that you are indeed a proficient writer. All of these speak to the future, not to what you've already done. Copyright protects the work you've already done, but your career will be based on the work that lies ahead.

In practical terms, copyright is, for you the creator, a way to protect yourself against people who might take your work (the protectable parts) without payment. In a sense, copyright is protection for weak creative people who need legal sanctions to shield them. By definition, a successful screenwriter is someone who repeatedly is employed as a writer for hire. When you look at the arc of a writer's career, you will find that the overwhelming majority of screenplays written on spec are by people new to the business, who are seeking to be recognized and hired. Once screenwriters are successful, they seldom risk months (or sometimes years) of their lives writing specs that nobody has asked for or offered payment for.[1]

Yes, this is a business of "who you know," but more importantly, it's a business of who knows you. Your work may be brilliant, but if no one knows about it, what value is it to you or anyone else?

How do others become aware of you? It is common for a new writer to achieve enough recognition to be approached by agents, managers, or sometimes even producers. Often, this takes place when the writer wins a screenwriting competition, or writes or directs a short, a webisode, or even a no-budget independent film that gets some attention.

This often leads to the writer's being invited to lunch. At that lunch, the agent, manager, producer, or development executive will frequently tell the new writer how much they "loved" the work but will often go on to say something like, "I just don't know how to sell it." This is followed by "What else do you have?"

Some writers conclude they were being lied to all along, and that the person praising them didn't really love their work. But if that's so, why would they bother to take you to lunch? They understand what you should understand— that it's not whether a work or its creator is loveable, it's whether enough people will see it so that its production costs represent a rational investment.

Often, the person who sought out the writer will describe a project they've optioned or purchased or merely have an interest in and ask the writer if they'd "like to take a crack at it?" Often, the agent or manager will want the writer to work for free, and new writers feel flattered to be asked and will accommodate the lunch buyer.

Working for free is in direct violation of the Writers Guild of America rules, but at this stage the new writer is not likely to be a member of the guild, because the principal way people get to join is to be hired by an entity the WGA recognizes and will do business with. This is pretty circular, but by now that shouldn't surprise you.

When someone asks a writer to work on their project, the writer might reply, "I want to work on *my* project, not somebody else's." The lunch will end, there will be a cordial handshake, but the writer still won't know how to pay the rent.

Ron Bass, a very successful screenwriter, was once asked at a WGA event how to deal with this dilemma. His response was, "Find your film inside their film." Very sage advice.

The reality is that the vast majority of human beings make their living by doing what somebody else wants them to do, not what they want to do. It would be nice if all creative people could live their lives composing only what they want to. Most, however, seldom enjoy that luxury.

WHY WRITE?

Writing is inherently risky. Many writers think that the biggest risk is that they're wasting their time because they're writing a project for a payoff that will never come. In monetary terms, that is often true.

But what exactly is your expected payoff? Why do you write a spec?

- For self-exploration;
- To exorcise demons;
- To sell the script;
- For self-production (writer as producer);
- For self-filming (writer as auteur)?

Clearly, the first two are solely for personal growth and artistic fulfillment. Neither finding an audience nor monetizing the project is a necessary component to either of these.

But once you move past the personal and into the commercial realm, your career most certainly does require finding an and selling to an audience.

When you write a spec—strike that—*before* you write a spec, ask yourself why you're doing it. There should always be some personal reason at the core—otherwise there probably is no core.

Are you writing for practice, as a calling card sample, or to sell? Certainly that should be the proper order of your expectations with a spec. It is always for practice. If the spec is good enough, you can use is as a writing sample to show around town. And there's the outside chance that if the stars align, literally and figuratively, you might sell the spec.

Selling doesn't happen often, but it does happen.

Writers should always gain a sense of personal satisfaction from self-exploration or exorcised demons or otherwise from their writing. We write from the personal for the personal. The rest is just business.

TO INFINITY AND BEYOND

If you want a profession, you must become professional. And that involves education. Learning the craft. Learning the traditions and conventions.

All of us, when we start this adventure, start it because we fall in love with great films, films that are so good that their execution looks effortless. And we want to get in on the fun. So we write our first scripts, and they are flawed but promising. We're disappointed. We're challenged. We learn more and more.

We write more scripts, and they're flawed in ways that are more subtle. We're frustrated. We feel abject. Where did the fun go?

We try to learn more, and maybe do, but that doesn't solve the problems. We have gained skill but lost heart.

We give up.

We go elsewhere.

Then we start again.

We let go of the learning by internalizing it. It moves from our heads to our hearts. And we're back to the love.

Now you're ready.

That is, in our opinion, the process of becoming a professional writer.

We wish you the very best of prolific travels.

APPENDIX A

Copyright Fundamentals

This appendix is in question-and-answer format to address the most common questions about rights and remedies under the copyright laws of the United States.

WHAT IS COPYRIGHT?

Copyright is your property right to your own writing. As the name implies, it is the right that gives you remedies against others if they copy from you without your permission. As courts and commentators have often said, copyright gives you a *monopoly* in the ownership of your writing.

Like other property rights, copyright flows from the United States Constitution. Ironically, though, when we were considering *Creativity and Copyright* as a title for this book, we were reminded that neither "creativity" nor "copyright" is a term found anywhere in the Constitution.

You read that correctly: there is no copyright clause in the Constitution. Instead, there is what is commonly called the Progress Clause. The Progress Clause gives Congress the authority to regulate intellectual property, including "writings":

> Congress shall have the power . . . To promote *the Progress* of Science and useful Arts, by securing for limited Times to Authors and Inventors the exclusive Right to their respective *Writings* and Discoveries. [emphasis added][1]

Writers may be surprised to learn that the Constitutional statement dealing with intellectual property is more concerned with art than commerce. The expressly stated goal is to "promote" the "arts," not to promote the careers of authors. Only in furtherance of promoting the arts are authors granted rights to their writings. And even then, the rights are not permanent.

How does this limited protection for writers promote the writing industry?

Before commerce, there was only patronage. That is, before there was a commercial market for publications, there were only individual patrons. A writer was paid if he had a rich patron paying him to write. Payment was a one-off, with no continuing rights to the work or residuals for republication. Often, the patron commissioned the work not for the text per se, but for a secondary use, such as an oral reading at a royal court or a performance in the theater.

But with the invention and spread of the printing press, words on paper started to become a tangible commercial product. Indeed, the first copyright-type laws were written to protect book publishers from unauthorized knock-offs.[2] Writers no longer had to rely on finding patrons. Instead, they found publishers who would distribute their works to a paying readership. In this new commercial model, the collective audience became the patron.

The United States Constitution recognizes the inherent tension between what's good for the creative industry as a whole versus what's good for any particular artist. If artists don't create, then there is no creative industry. So artists are granted exclusive rights to their work, but not forever.

As writers and idea purveyors, we take comfort in knowing that the framers of our Constitution cared about creativity and wanted to promote it. But they also provided that the monopoly power ("the exclusive right") granted by the Constitution had an important condition—it was "for limited times."

Congress first exercised its power under the Progress Clause by enacting the federal Copyright Act in 1790. As with all statutory bodies of law, the Copyright Act is subject to amendment and change. Significant amendments were made in 1831, 1909, 1976, and 1998. The most recent changes to the Copyright Act have largely been prompted by commercial entities seeking to maximize their profits by extending the term of copyright protection.

When the framers of the Constitution drafted the Progress Clause, they were not thinking about radio, television, or movies. Nor were they thinking about computers, software, or the internet. Just as the invention of certain media at the beginning of the twentieth century presented intellectual property challenges, so does the cyber revolution now.

Media changes, but the balancing of interests remains the same: On the one hand, the Constitution proposes that society has a vested interest in encouraging creativity, and one way to accomplish this is to give creators time to profit from their work. On the other hand, society also has a vested interest in making it possible for everyone to use what has been created, to incorporate individual creations into the common pool of knowledge, art, and science available for all to use without restriction.

These two principles reveal the balancing act that has always marked copyright. This balancing act is at the heart of all copyright disputes.

WHAT DOES COPYRIGHT PROTECT?

Copyright protects your "*original* works of authorship fixed in any tangible medium of expression." (emphasis added).[3] That phrase, quoted directly from the Copyright Act, seems clear enough. In other words, your original writing.

But that's where much confusion begins. A plain-language interpretation could be disastrously misleading, because "original" is not plain language in this context; it is a term of legal art.

When the copyright law says "original," it is not referring to newness or uniqueness or artistic quality. "Original" in copyright law refers only to the source—you—and means *original to you*. "Original" means you wrote it yourself; that is, you didn't copy it from anywhere.

WHAT ARE THE "RIGHTS" OF COPYRIGHT?

Copyright, as the name implies, is the exclusive right to copy. The copyright owner of a script has the exclusive right to do any of the following:

1. copy the script;[4]
2. sell, license, or option the script;[5]
3. make "derivative" projects from the script, such as filming a motion picture of the script, basing a television series on it, and developing prequels, sequels, spin-offs, or novelizations based on the script;[6]
4. show or perform the script publicly.[7]

You, as the copyright owner, can *authorize* others to exercise any or all of these rights. Correspondingly, you can *prevent* others from exercising any of these rights without your authorization.

For violation of any of these rights, there are certain statutory remedies.[8] A violation—also referred to as an *infringement*[9]—is both civilly actionable and criminally punishable. In a civil court, the copyright holder may bring a claim for injunctive relief and money damages against an infringer. In federal criminal court, the government may prosecute infringers and impose monetary fines and jail time.

WHAT'S THE DIFFERENCE BETWEEN COPYRIGHT INFRINGEMENT AND PLAGIARISM?

Copyright infringement is copying someone else's copyrighted material without their permission. Copyright is a personal property violation and a criminal wrong.

Key: Don't use someone's words without permission.

Plagiarism is an academic impropriety. Plagiarism is passing off someone else's ideas as your own. A plagiarist could also be a copyright infringer by using verbatim excerpts without authorization and attribution. Paraphrasing the source material gets you past infringement, but if you pass the ideas off as your own and don't properly acknowledge the source material, then you're a plagiarist.

Key: Don't use someone's ideas without attribution.

HOW DOES A WRITER GET A COPYRIGHT?

By writing. Writers just need to write. *Nothing more, but nothing less.*

Nothing more: Copyright is secured automatically the instant a work is created. And a work is created when it is fixed in any tangible form, such as ink on paper or data saved on an electronic device (e.g., on your hard drive or on a server in the cloud). Fixed, for most of us, simply means hitting "save." That's it. You do not need publication, registration, or any other action to secure your statutory copyright.

But nothing less: If you talk (and talk and talk) about your story but never get it written down in any tangible form, then it simply is not protected by copyright. For example, and perhaps most significantly, oral pitches are not protected by copyright. (More about the dilemma of pitching in chapter 4, "Selling to Others.") Copyright does not protect mere oral expression.

You get the rights when you write.

DO I NEED TO USE A © SYMBOL ON MY WORK FOR PROTECTION?

No, not after March 1, 1989.[10] Since then, the use of a copyright symbol or any other such copyright notice is no longer required.

Under prior law, an author was required to place on the work (1) the copyright symbol or the word "copyright," (2) the first year of publication, if any, and (3) the name of the copyright owner. For example:

unpublished: Unpublished work © 2019 Jay Gee
published: © 2019 Jay Gee

However, the advice many lawyers would give you is that even though copyright notice is no longer required, including it may still benefit writers. Doing so informs the public that the script is protected by copyright, identifies the copyright owner, and shows the first date of publication. And there really is no disadvantage. You don't need permission from the US Copyright Office and it costs you nothing to include the notice, so it's generally good advice.

But not for screenwriters.

We've noticed that professional scripts passed around inside the industry among managers, agents, producers, directors, and actors *never* have a copyright notice. It just isn't done. Industry professionals know that scripts are protected by copyright. A copyright notice comes off as a little too precious, a little too paranoid. A little too amateurish.

Don't lose credibility with your reader with your spec's cover page. Be a pro. Go forth confidently without a copyright notice.

WHEN DOES MY COPYRIGHT START?

The instant you put your words into a tangible medium (e.g., ink on the page or hitting "save" on your electronic device), copyright protection begins.

HOW LONG DOES COPYRIGHT LAST?

Copyright lasts through the author's lifetime and for 70 years afterward.[11]

The debate over how long a copyright should last is as old as the oldest copyright statute, and it will doubtless continue as long as there is a copyright law.[12]

The first United States copyright statute, enacted in 1790, provided a federal copyright term of twenty-eight years (fourteen years from the date of publication, renewable for an additional fourteen if the author survived the first term).[13] In 1831, Congress expanded the term to forty-two years (twenty-eight years from publication, renewable for an additional fourteen years).[14] And in 1909, it increased it to fifty-six years (twenty-eight years from publication, renewable for an additional twenty-eight).[15]

In 1976, Congress altered the method for computing federal copyright terms. The 1976 act provided that federal copyright protection would run from the work's creation, not—as in the 1790, 1831, and 1909 acts—its publication. Protection would last until fifty years after the author's death.[16] In these respects, the 1976 act aligned United States copyright terms with the then-dominant international standard adopted under the Berne Convention for the Protection of Literary and Artistic Works.

In 1998, the Copyright Term Extension Act, more commonly referred to as the CTEA—also respectfully known as the Sonny Bono Copyright Term Extension Act, or derisively as the Mickey Mouse Protection Act—installed the fourth major enlargement of federal copyright duration.[17] CTEA enlarges the terms of all existing and future copyrights by twenty years. For works created by identified natural persons, the term now lasts from creation until seventy years after the author's death.[18]

This CTEA standard harmonizes the baseline United States copyright term with the term adopted by the European Union in 1993.[19]

DO I HAVE TO REGISTER MY SCRIPT WITH THE COPYRIGHT OFFICE TO GET COPYRIGHT PROTECTION?

No, absolutely not. For scripts and other works written on or after January 1, 1978, registration is no longer a pre-condition of copyright protection.[20] Nevertheless, there are still definite advantages to copyright registration, particularly in the litigation context.

First, you must register before you can maintain a lawsuit against an infringer.[21]

Second, if your registration was made before publication or within five years of publication, your name on the registration certificate is accepted by the court as prima facie evidence that you are the copyright holder.[22] That's an advantage for you in a lawsuit.

Third, if registration is made within three months of publication or before any infringement, then the copyright holder is entitled to statutory damages as well as attorney's fees.[23] This right to attorney's fees is a tremendous strategic advantage, and in and of itself is a compelling reason for writers to register their work.

Finally, there's really no reason not to register. Registration is cheap and easy and fast. After you're done with all your rewrites but before you start submitting your script around town, simply register it with the Copyright Office.

WHAT IS THE EFFECTIVE DATE OF COPYRIGHT REGISTRATION?

Copyright registration is effective on the date that the Copyright Office receives each of the following:[24]

1. the completed application form,
2. a nonrefundable application fee, and
3. a true and correct deposit copy of the script. For unpublished scripts (e.g., the typical spec script), only one copy is required. For published scripts, two copies are required.

As you'll note, your registration is effective well before the date when you actually get a registration certificate back from the Copyright Office.

WHAT VALUE IS THERE IN A COPYRIGHT REGISTRATION CERTIFICATE?

When the Copyright Office issues a certificate to you, it means only that

1. your application form was filled out completely,
2. your payment cleared for the registration fee, and
3. your work falls in one of the categories that copyright law is authorized to protect, namely literary works or motion pictures.[25]

Issuance of the certificate does *not* mean that the Copyright Office has analyzed the contents of your work for originality. Large portions of your work may be unprotectable (e.g., they belong to the public domain). Portions might even infringe on another's copyright. That's all invisible to the Copyright Office when it issues a registration certificate.

IS WGA REGISTRATION A SUBSTITUTE FOR COPYRIGHT REGISTRATION?

No. WGA registration is *not* a substitute for copyright registration, but it is still useful to register with the Writers Guild. We recommend that you register with both.

The Writers Guild of America is a custodian of records service that proves that your script existed as of the registration date. Why is the date important? Because if your script did not physically exist in the world before someone else's did, they could not have copied yours. It would be a physical impossibility. So you need to show that yours was first-in-time.

Here's how WGA registration works:

You deposit a copy of your script with the WGA, either hard copy or a digital version, and pay a nominal registration fee. For hard copy registration, the WGA places the script in an envelope, seals the envelope, labels the envelope with your registration information (writer's name, script name, registration number, etc.), enters the registration information into its database, issues a certificate of registration to you, and deposits the envelope in the WGA vault. Electronic registration is similar, with retention of your script in a secure WGA database.

The WGA will retain the deposited script for five years, with another five-year renewal option. If called upon, the WGA will appear at any evidentiary hearing (official guild action, arbitration, or trial) with the registered script and provide authentication that the script existed in the deposited form as of the date of registration.

WGA registration shows that your script was in existence before an infringer's script. If your script is first-in-time, then it's possible that the infringer could have had access to it. On the other hand, if your script was written after theirs was, how could they have copied yours? Not possible. Therefore, it is important to establish that your script was first-in-time. (See chapter 5, "Copyright Infringement.")

WGA registration is probably most effective for affording quick and easy access to scripts in order to establish authorship for screen credits in guild arbitration. Again, the WGA registry is a custodial service.

The Copyright Office function is much broader. As noted above, you absolutely must register with the Copyright Office before you can maintain a lawsuit against an infringer. (If you file a lawsuit without a registered copyright, the federal court will dismiss your case and send you away until you do register.) Also, timely copyright registration gives you a statutory right to recover your attorney's fees from an infringer. And believe us, having the other side reimburse you for your attorney's fees is a significant right.

WHAT IS A "POOR MAN'S COPYRIGHT"?

We suppose that as long as there's a United States Postal Service, there will be the myth of the poor man's copyright.

The so-called poor man's copyright is not a copyright at all. You get a poor man's copyright by mailing a copy of your script to yourself. When the package with the script arrives, you don't open it; instead, you store it in your file cabinet. Then, if there is ever a dispute about authorship, at the time of arbitration or trial, you open the mailed envelope before the arbitrator or judge and jury (perhaps with much suspense and drama?) to show conclusively that your script existed as of the date post-marked on the envelope. Does that matter?

Yes. Because no one ever admits copying, and no one is ever caught red-handed in the act of copying, there's never any direct evidence of copying in a copyright infringement law-suit. Copying is always shown, if at all, by circumstantial evidence. And a key circumstantial fact is which script was first in time.

If yours was first, the other party conceivably could have copied you. But if theirs was first, it's physically impossible that they copied you.

Does this sound familiar?

Of course it does. The poor man's copyright method is, in effect, using the U.S. Postal Service instead of the WGA as the custodian of records for your script. This quaint method sounds like something out of a 1940s film noir. Perhaps that's its charm for some writers. But in the parlance of film noir, "Cute. Too cute for your own good."

Federal postal workers are not in the business of showing up at trial to authenticate canceled postmarks on envelopes. You would have to issue a subpoena and tender witness fees to the Postal Service to get a worker to appear. And how would you establish that your envelope had not been tampered with while it was in your possession? If challenged, you would need to hire a forensic expert to examine the envelope and testify in court as to its untampered condition.

You get the idea. A poor man's copyright could become awk-ward and expensive. Pick the proper tool for the job. The post office is not in the custodian-of-records business for screenplays and is, at best, a very awkward fit for the job.

Much better to register with the WGA.

SHOULD I USE A PRIVATE CUSTODIAN COMPANY
FOR SCRIPT REGISTRATION?

No. Yikes, no.

From time to time, we see a few private custodian companies advertise on the web, offering to perform what is basically the same custodial function that the WGA offers. We aren't commenting on the integrity of those companies or the quality of their professional service, much less passing judgment on any company in particular. But we do want to comment on the practice generally.

The private custodial companies we've seen are simply lawyers or law firms trying to branch into a new business line: lawyers offering to wear a custodian-of-records hat.

Rather than an employee from the WGA registry, the lawyer will appear in court for you as the custodian. And we know how much juries like lawyers! Better to use the more likeable and less expensive professionals who perform this service routinely for the industry.

Use the WGA registry.

WHO IS THE "AUTHOR" OF A SCRIPT
UNDER COPYRIGHT LAW?

The term "writer" is not found anywhere is the Copyright Act. Instead, the act speaks in terms of "author." Of course, the writer is usually the author.

Indeed, the general rule is that the writer who wrote the script holds the copyright to that script.[26] (And cowriters are coauthors, unless there is an agreement between them to the contrary.) This general rule applies most typically to projects written on spec.

But not all writing is done on spec. A common exception to this general rule is work made for hire.[27]

WHAT IS "WORK MADE FOR HIRE"?

In the screenwriting context, a work made for hire is a script that is "specially ordered or commissioned." That is to say, someone else is paying you to write the script. You're under contract. Congratulations!

In a work-for-hire situation, that other paying party is the "author" and copyright owner, not you, the writer.

This, of course, makes commercial sense—on the one side is the copyright, on the other side is the money. The nature of the legal relationship dictates who holds which. When you write on spec, the copyright is yours until you're paid to transfer it to a buyer. When you're working for hire, you've already been paid (or promised you'll be paid upon delivery) and the copyright goes to the party who commissioned you to write. It's simply a question of when you've sold your script and the accompanying copyright— after you've written it (spec) or before you write it (work for hire).

It is important to note in the screenwriting context that the paying party does not need to be—and usually is not—the writer's employer.[28] The writer maintains independent contractor status and is not an employee of the studio or production company or whoever else has commissioned the script.

By the time you see a film in the theater or on a home screen, the "writer" is no longer legally the "author." That is because the writer has long since signed away his or her rights to the work. If you look at the last frame of the credits, it will state that, for copyright law purposes, the studio or distributor is the author of this work. The writer gets "written by" credit, but not an authorship designation.

Before you sell your spec script, you are legally the copyright holder. But when you sell your script to a production company, you sign a sale and transfer of your copyright, and for any rewrites or polishes that you are retained to perform going forward, you sign a document acknowledging that you are now a "writer for hire." So you give up all ownership and control of your work.

CAN I COPYRIGHT THE TITLE OF MY SCRIPT?

No. Copyright does not protect titles.[29]

The courts have concluded that mere titles contain too little "expression" for protection.[30] Similarly, copyright does not protect names, short phrases, or slogans.

But that does not mean that titles, names, short phrases, and slogans are completely unprotectable or unprotected. Film titles may be protected by trademark law, trade association rules, or private contract.

MPAA Registration

All the major film studios are member of the Motion Picture Association of America.[31] The MPAA is the trade association for American film, and it maintains a registry of film titles. A member may register a title for its exclusive use, and that registration is enforceable against all other members and precludes them from using the same title.

Trademark Protection

Similarly, an exception to the general principle that you can't copyright a title is the concept/doctrine of "secondary meaning": that is, the title is so closely associated with a particular story that it becomes almost synonymous to that story. It's like the way we refer to all tissues as Kleenex no matter what brand they actually are.

We wouldn't advise someone to make a film called *Gone with the Wind* (Best Picture, 1939 Academy Awards). The author of *The Wind Done Gone* (a 2001 novel retelling the events of *Gone with the Wind* from the point of view of a slave) spent a lot of time and money fending off the litigation brought by the estate of Margaret Mitchell before agreeing to make a confidential donation to Morehouse College to settle the lawsuit.

Best Practice: Mum's the Word?

What about your unpublished spec script with a really great title?

That would fall into the gap in protection between copyright law (which does not protect titles) and trademark law (which only protects well-known titles with secondary meaning in the market). That gap can be significant and problematic for a spec writer.

If a writer has a really great and unique title, but the underlying literary property is not published, or is published but doesn't become popular enough to give rise to a secondary meaning, then the author's really great title is up for grabs, free for the taking.

Perhaps this explains why many studio projects are referenced in the trades as, for example, an "Untitled Michael Mann Project." It is bad strategy to put the title out there without the underlying literary project. The title only gains protection through the success and popularity of the literary product.

Where does this leave the spec script writer who submits an okay script with a really great title? Screwed, perhaps.

Better to submit only great scripts.

IS MY COPYRIGHT EFFECTIVE IN OTHER COUNTRIES?

Unfortunately, intellectual property laws are not universal.[32] At least not yet.

Copyright is territorial. That means that a United States copyright does not exist outside the United States. Nevertheless, the United States has commercial relations with most countries throughout the world, including arrangements for the worldwide distribution of Hollywood films.

The Berne Convention, to which the United States became a signatory effective March 1, 1989, is a multinational treaty establishing reciprocal intellectual property rights among 140 countries. Countries that are signatories to the convention apply the protection of their intellectual property laws to the works of authors from other member countries. For example, if your spec were to be infringed on by a filmmaker in Paris, because France is a Berne signatory, the French courts would give you intellectual property protection under the laws of that country.

So are you protected? In a nutshell, you do have intellectual property protection in other countries. But that protection depends upon

- the existence of a mutual treaty, such as Berne, between the United States and the country where the infringement occurred, and
- the laws in the country of infringement (not U.S. copyright laws).

The complexities of international intellectual property protection are much more important for studios and distributors than they are for the spec screenwriter. Unless you're doing a lot of Skype pitches or otherwise taking meetings outside the United States, this is probably not a concern for you.

Collaboration Problems

WHEN A COWRITER DOESN'T WRITE

We present a hypothetical situation that, unfortunately, is not uncommon, particularly among writers early in their careers. (Of course, this is a hypothetical, and "any resemblance to actual persons, living or dead, or actual events, is purely coincidental.")

We have the writers as being friends from film school, but the preexisting relationship could be from internships, day jobs, or night haunts. The concept is that these are two acquaintances with similar sensibilities who want to do a spec project together. Our running analysis explores your rights and remedies as a writer whose cowriter doesn't write.

You and Guy went to film school together. Upon graduation, you and Guy decide to collaborate on creating some films projects.

So far so good. Films school gives you a common language and common history. And since you have a preexisting relationship, there is a good chance that your existing relationship will be at least as important as your future projects.

Because neither of you has any money to purchase or option scripts, you decided to write your own scripts together.

Bravo! The best equity is sweat equity.

Guy had been a producing student, and you a screenwriting student.

You and Guy should be very candid about your expectations from each other. It's certainly acceptable for collaborators to come to the table with different skill sets, as long as all parties know what to expect in advance. Will you be the lead writer? Will you have to teach Guy screenwriting? Will Guy teach you the business moves of producing in exchange?

Also, you should do your due diligence. A producing student likely knows story, but does he have any writing chops? Has Guy, in fact, ever written? If so, have you read his writing samples?

You and Guy meet regularly each week, and generate a list of 150 project titles. The energy and momentum in the room is wonderful. So wonderful that you don't bother with negotiating and signing a written collaboration agreement because you don't want to buzz kill the room with legal talk.

The first thing you and Guy write together should be a collaboration agreement that captures your mutual expectations about participation and results. The best time to reach agreement is when the team is fresh and excited and agreeable. And certainly before problems start.[1]

The list of projects is probably nothing more than mere unprotected ideas. But the list and the meetings are evidence of the collaborative relationship, even in the absence of an express oral or written contract.

Guy keeps the list on his hard drive, and puts a copyright notice on the bottom on the list: © 2019 Guy.

The titles individually, and the list of titles collectively, are not protectable by copyright, so the copyright notice has no legal effect. But it is perhaps a red flag that Guy is self-dealing, in violation of your collaboration agreement.

You did not keep a list.

A bad practice. Not fatal, but potentially problematic with regard to proof of your participation.

One of the projects on the list is a story called "Red Rabbit Run." You and Guy talked about the story a lot, and even met with one of Guy's friends, a junior studio executive, who gave you both input on the story.

Talking isn't writing, but it is collaborating. A benefit of relationships is extended relationships. Your coauthor's contacts are now your contacts too. So Guy has brought a resource to the table.

Be a bit watchful about the studio friend potentially glomming on to the project.

Although you and Guy agreed to cowrite the story, Guy simply was not a writer. So you wrote act 1. Then act 3. You sent these to Guy, but Guy still didn't write anything. Finally, out of frustration, you completed the script.

Ugh. Welcome to a bad collaboration. You are now alone together. In the majority of places (including, especially, California and New York), you would be considered the sole author. The majority rule requires that collaborators

· intended to be coauthors, and
· have each independently made copyrightable contributions to the work.[2]

Let's look at this in the context of you and Guy.

INTENT. As the lawyers would say, the parties must "entertain in their minds the concept of joint authorship" such that the "participants fully intend to be joint authors." This element "is not strictly subjective," however, and "does not turn solely on the parties' own words and professed state of mind." Rather, "a more nuanced inquiry into the factual indicia of ownership and authorship" is required, "such as how a collaborator regarded [him]self in relation to the work in terms of billing and credit, decision-making, and the right to enter into contracts."[3]

In plain language: Did you discuss being coauthors? Did you agree to be coauthors? Do you have a signed collaboration agreement that says you'll be coauthors? Do the drafts of the script have both your names on them? Have you referred to yourselves as coauthors in reaching out to any third parties (e.g., in inquiry letters to managers, agents, actors, directors, producers)? These are the facts that would evidence your intent or lack of intent.

It seems that you and Guy did intend to be coauthors. You discussed working together. You met with at least one development executive as a team. You generated a list of projects together. It sounds like you intended to collaborate. The fact that you never captured your intent expressly in a written collaboration agreement is not a deal killer. You seemed to perform and hold yourselves out as a team.

COPYRIGHTABLE CONTRIBUTION. As the lawyers would say, there is no requirement that "the several authors must necessarily work in physical propinquity, or in concert, nor that the respective contributions made by each joint author must be equal either in quantity or quality."[4]

In plain language: You don't have to write in the same place, or write at the same time, or write equal amounts, or write equally well to be collaborators.

But you both do need to be writing. Because if you're not an author, then you can't be a coauthor. Collaboration alone is insufficient to establish joint authorship. Each purported joint author must have contributed copyrightable expression to the work.

The fact that you—and only you—performed the writing cuts strongly in your favor on this second prong. It sounds like you and Guy intended a collaboration, but Guy failed to collaborate. It seems you're the sole author under copyright law.

Caveat: that's the majority rule (in California and New York, most prominently).[5] There is a minority view (in Chicago) that mere intent alone is legally sufficient for a finding of coauthorship.

Guy registers the spec with the Copyright Office in his own name as sole author.

Wow. Under no legal theory is Guy the sole author. That's just a bad faith registration.

Who can legally register a copyright? Only the following:

1. the actual writer(s);
2. the employer who has retained the writer(s) under a work-for-hire relationship (usually a producer or the studio); or
3. someone who received a written transfer of copyright from 1 or 2.

Categories 2 and 3 clearly do not apply to Guy, so his only theory for copyright ownership would be under category 1. But copyright ownership ordinarily vests in the person who actually creates the work. Guy did not actually write anything. Guy might assert that he has coauthorship rights because you and he were operating under a handshake (oral) collaboration agreement and intended that the spec be treated as a work of coauthorship.

In the majority of places, including California (Ninth Circuit) and New York (Second Circuit), that would not be sufficient, because each must contribute independently copyrightable writing. But in Chicago (Seventh Circuit), it might be sufficient, because the intent to have a joint work is the controlling factor (not the copyrightability of any contributions).

Those are the default rules that apply in those jurisdictions when there is no written collaboration agreement squarely addressing the parties' intention, or if the collaboration agreement is silent on the issue. That's why it's important to use a written collaboration agreement that clearly sets out the rules of the relationship, especially what will constitute coauthorship. And, if one of the parties is not living up to the deal, it is equally important to formally end the relationship with a written termination.

In our hypothetical situation, that would have been the only way that you could have cleanly moved forward solo. Guy will argue that although he did not write anything, he contributed ideas orally, and that you both intended this to be his contribution for coauthorship.

You sold the spec to a producer for $1,000. But Guy now claims that he should get all the money. And more: Guy claims that the fair market value of the script was $65,000 and he is entitled to all of that.

This is when the loose ends of the collaboration relationship come back to haunt you. All the money? No, Guy is not entitled to all the money. You are, at the very least, a co-owner of the script. Either co-owner can sell the script without permission from the other.

Half the money? At best, Guy is entitled to his 50 percent share under the collaboration relationship. Although Guy did not write anything, he did bring certain resources to the table during the development process and in furtherance of the collaboration.

None of the money? Yes. Because you're the sole author, you should get the sole paycheck.

More money? What if the script were, in fact, worth $20,000? Or what if the producer were a signatory to the WGA and therefore guild minimum applied? So you made a bad deal? You sold for too little.

That's the risk that collaborators face—that one of them might unilaterally make a bad deal, and both have to live with it. That's why your written collaboration agreement should require that both parties must sign off on any sale.

What if you deliberately undersold the project just to spite Guy? It was worth it for you to take a loss just so Guy would take a loss? If you acted in bad faith, then Guy might claim that you breached the collaboration agreement. And Guy might be right.

Better to close out the relationship before you close out the sale.

Notes

INTRODUCTION

1. U.S. Const. art. I, § 8. Traditionally, this was referred to as the Progress Clause, but it is now sometimes called the Copyright Clause, the Patent Clause, or the Intellectual Property Clause.

CHAPTER ONE. FREE FOR THE TAKING

1. Berkic v. Crichton (9th Cir. 1985) 761 F.2d 1289, *cert. denied,* 474 U.S. 826, 88 L.Ed.2d 69, 106 S. Ct. 85 (1985).
2. 17 U.S.C. § 105.
3. Hoehling v. Universal City Studios, Inc. (2nd Cir. 1980) 618 F.2d 972, 978. Speculation about history is not protected by copyright, no matter how creative and new. You're layering your speculation—which you're asserting as a true theory—on top of public domain facts.
4. 17 U.S.C. § 102(b).
5. Desny v. Wilder (1956) 46 Cal.2d 715, 731–732 (ideas are free as the air). For more, see chapter 4, "Selling to Others."
6. "Spike Lee's Timely Period Piece," *Wall Street Journal,* Aug. 9, 2018, page A9.

7. Nichols v. Universal Pictures Corporation (2nd Cir. 1930) 45 F.2d 119, 121–122.

8. *Nichols*, supra.

9. *Nichols*, supra. See also Sid & Marty Krofft Television Productions, Inc. v. McDonald's Corp. (9th Cir. 1977) 562 F.2d 1157, 1163–1164.

10. *Krofft*, 562 F.2d at 1164.

11. *Krofft*, 562 F.2d at 1163.

12. Schwarz v. Universal Pictures Co. (S.D. Cal. 1945) 85 F. Supp. 270, 275.

13. 17 U.S.C. § 107.

14. Id.

CHAPTER TWO. CLEARANCE REQUIRED

1. See chapter 1, "Free for the Taking."

2. See chapter 1, "Free for the Taking."

3. Anderson v. Stallone, 11 U.S.P.Q.2d (BNA) 1161.

4. De Havilland v. FX Networks, LLC (2018) 21 Cal.App.5th 845, 849–850; Sarver v. Chartier (9th Cir. 2016) 813 F.3d 891, 903–906.

5. Cal. Civ. Code § 3344 (right of publicity—all living persons).

6. Cal. Civ. Code § 3344.1 (right of publicity—deceased celebrities).

7. U.S. Const. art I, § 8.

8. *Sarver*, 813 F.3d at 905; Polydors v. Twentieth Century Fox Film Corp. (1998) 67 Cal.App.4th 318, 323–325.

9. Comedy III Productions, Inc. v. Gary Saderup, Inc. (2001) 25 Cal.4th 387, *cert. denied*, 534 U.S. 1078, 122 S.Ct. 806, 151 L.Ed.2d 692.

10. Hilton v. Hallmark Cards (9th Cir. 2010) 599 F.3d 894.

11. Davis v. Electronic Arts, Inc. (9th Cir. 2015) 775 F.3d 1172.

12. Abdul-Jabbar v. GMC (9th Cir. 1996) 75 F.3d 1391; Downing v. Ambercrombie & Fitch (9th Cir. 2001) 265 F.3d 994.

13. Cal. Civ. Code § 3344.1(a)(2) ("For purposes of this subdivision, a play, book, magazine, newspaper, musical composition, audiovisual work, radio or television program, single and original work of art, work of political or newsworthy value, or an advertisement or commercial announcement for any of these works, shall not be considered a product, article of merchandise, good, or service if it is fictional or nonfictional entertainment, or a dramatic, literary, or musical work.")

CHAPTER THREE. COLLABORATION

1. When the studio hires a string of successive writers, is that collaboration? No, not in the traditional sense that results in coauthorship under the copyright act. In fact, the author in that context is the studio that has employed a string of work-for-hire writers. The writers don't work together, they work consecutively.

2. 17 U.S.C. § 101.

3. 17 U.S.C. § 201(a).

4. 17 U.S.C. § 201; Weissmann v. Freeman (2nd Cir. 1989) 868 F.2d 1313, 1318.

5. 17 U.S.C. § 204(a).

6. 17 U.S.C. § 204(a).

7. Time, Inc. v. Kastner (S.D.N.Y. 1997) 972 F.Supp. 236, 238 (17 U.S.C. § 204(a) bars breach of contract claims based on oral agreements); see also Konigsberg Int'l, Inc. v. Rice (9th Cir. 1994) 16 F.3d 355, 358 (cannot "dispense with the written instrument requirement altogether by claiming an oral partnership or joint venture").

8. See Robinson v. Buy-Rite Costume Jewelry, Inc., 2004 U.S. Dist. LEXIS 11542, *fees denied,* 2004 U.S. Dist. LEXIS 16675.

9. Aalmuhammed v. Lee (9th Cir. 2000) 202 F.3d 1227, 1235.

10. See www.wga.org/contracts/credits/manuals for WGA rules regarding writers' credits.

11. Childress v. Taylor (2nd Cir. 1991) 945 F.2d 500, 507; Ashton-Tate Corp. v. Ross (9th Cir. 1990) 916 F.2d 516, 521.

12. *Childress,* 945 F.2d at 508–509. But see *Nimmer on Copyright* § 6.07[A][3][a], at 22, suggesting that each author's contribution need not be copyrightable. The key is the intent of the parties at the time the work is done.

13. Thomson v. Larson (2nd Cir. 1998) 147 F.3d 195, 206.

14. *Nimmer on Copyright* § 6.03, at 7. Each author's contribution, however, must be more than de minimis. Id., § 6.07[A][1], at 21.

15. *Childress,* 945 F.2d at 508–509.

CHAPTER FOUR. SELLING TO OTHERS

1. *Harvard Business Review,* September 2015, pp. 107, 128.

2. Desny v. Wilder (1956) 46 Cal.2d 715.

3. *Desny,* 46 Cal.2d at 727.

4. Benay v. Warner Bros. Entertainment, Inc. (9th Cir. 2010) 607 F.3d 620; *on remand summary judgment granted in part, denied in part,* 2012 U.S. Dist. LEXIS 183791.

5. *Desny,* 46 Cal.2d at 733–734. The studio is paying for the disclosure of the idea. Therefore, the act of pitching is itself a professional service. If, as a result of your professional service, the studio uses your idea, then it is implied that you will be compensated.

CHAPTER FIVE. COPYRIGHT INFRINGEMENT

1. Steven T. Lowe, "The Death of Copyright," *Los Angeles Lawyer,* November 2010; see also Steven T. Lowe and Daniel Lifschitz, "The Death of Copyright, the Sequel," *Computer & Internet Lawyer* 29, no. 9 (September 2012).

2. Don't mistake a prima facie case with actually proving your case. A prima facie case is made (or not) early in the lawsuit, at the pleading phase. But actually proving your case with admissible evidence comes later. And you do indeed have the burden of proof. That means you have to come forward with

admissible evidence. Evidence to show what? Evidence to establish each element of the prima facie case.

3. Ford Motor Co. v. Summit Motor Productions (3rd Cir. 1991) 930 F2d 277, 299–300.

4. Educational Testing Service v. Simon (C.D. Cal. 1999) 95 F.Supp.2d 1081, 1087.

5. 17 U.S.C. §§ 106–122, 501(a).

6. Idema v. Dreamworks, Inc. (C.D. Cal. 2001) 162 F. Supp.2d 1129, 1135; see also Idema v. Dreamworks, Inc. (9th Cir. 2003) 90 Fed.Appx. 496 (summary judgment affirmed in an unpublished opinion).

7. 17 U.S.C. § 106.

8. Instruction 1.9, "Direct and Circumstantial Evidence," *Ninth Circuit Model Civil Jury Instructions,* www.akd. uscourts.gov/sites/akd/files/model_jury_civil.pdf.

9. Id.

10. Id.

11. Three Boys Music Corp. v. Bolton, 212 F.3d 477, 482 (9th Cir. 2000) (quoting Sid & Marty Krofft Television Productions, Inc. v. McDonald's Corp. (9th Cir. 1977) 562 F.2d 1157, 1172), *cert. denied,* 2001 U.S. LEXIS 800.

12. Jason v. Fonda (9th Cir. 1982) 698 F.2d 966, 967, *incorporating by reference,* Jason v. Fonda (C.D. Cal. 1981) 526 F. Supp. 774.

13. Id.

14. Echevarria v. Warner Bros. Pictures, Inc. (S.D. Cal. 1935) 12 F.Supp. 632, 639; Warner Bros., Inc. v. American Broadcasting Companies, Inc. (2nd Cir. 1981) 654 F.2d 204.

15. Art Attacks Ink, LLC v. MGA Entertainment, Inc. (9th Cir. 2009) 581 F.3d 1138, 1145.

16. Jorgensen v. Epic/Sony Records (2nd Cir. 2003) 351 F.3d 46, 52–53; Meta-Film Association, Inc. v. MCA, Inc. (C.D. Cal. 1984), 586 F.Supp. 1346, 1358.

17. *Meta-Film,* 586 F.Supp at 1355–1356.

18. Baxter v. MCA, Inc. (9th Cir. 1987) 812 F.2d 421, 423, 423 n.2.

19. Walker v. University Books, Inc. (9th Cir. 1979) 602 F.2d 859, 864.

20. Feist Publications, Inc. v. Rural Telephone Service Co., Inc. (1991) 499 U.S. 340; 111 S.Ct. 1282, 1287; 113 L.Ed.2d 358.

21. We say "almost" because there could be a situation where a writer for hire sues his former employer claiming that the script written during their relationship was a spec script, not a work for hire. The work-for-hire script and the spec script could be identical because they are indeed the same script. The script is not the issue. The real issue is the status of the writer, i.e., whether a work-for-hire writer or an independent spec writer.

22. Klekas v. EMI Films (1984) 150 Cal.App.3d 1102, 1111; Weitzenkorn v. Lesser (1953) 40 Cal.2d 778, 791; Mann v. Columbia Pictures, Inc. (1982) 128 Cal.App.3d 628, 634; Apple Computers, Inc. v. Microsoft Corp. (9th Cir. 1994) 35 F.3d 1435, 1446.

23. *Idema,* 162 F.Supp.2d at 1176–1177, citing Kouf v. Walt Disney Pictures & TV (9th Cir. 1994) 16 F.3d 1042, 1045 and Shaw v. Lindheim (9th Cir. 1990) 919 F.3d 1353, 1359.

24. Benay v. Warner Bros. Entertainment, Inc. (9th Cir. 2010) 607 F.3d 620, 625–627.

25. Dr. Seuss Enterprises v. Penguin Books (9th Cir. 1997) 109 F.3d 1394, 1398.

26. Lowe, "Death of Copyright," p. 32.

27. Berkic v. Crichton (9th Cir. 1985) 761 F.2d 1289, 1292, *cert. denied,* 474 U.S. 826, 88 L.Ed.2d 69, 106 S. Ct. 85 (1985).

28. A seven-element extrinsic test (plot, themes, dialog, mood, setting, pace, sequence) first appeared in *Jason,* 698 F.2d 966. An eighth element (character) was added by Overman v. Universal City Studios, Inc. (C.D. Cal. 1984) 605 F.Supp. 350. These eight elements have been recited as an unchanged mantra by the Ninth Circuit since Litchfield v. Spielberg (9th Cir. 1984) 736 F.2d 1352, 1356, *cert. denied*, 470 U.S. 1052, 84 L. Ed. 2d 817, 105 S. Ct. 1753 (1985).

29. Christopher Booker, *The Seven Basic Plots: Why We Tell Stories* (New York: Continuum, 2004); Georges Polti, *The Thirty-Six Dramatic Situations* (San Diego: Book Tree, 2016).

30. Weygand v. CBS, Inc. (C.D. Cal. 1997) 43 U.S.P.Q.2d (BNA) 1120; Sony Pictures Entertainment, Inc. v. Fireworks Entertainment Group, Inc. (C.D. Cal. 2001) 156 F.Supp.2d 1148, *vacated*, 2002 U.S. Dist. LEXIS 28457 (vacated "in view of settlement by the parties"); *Idema*, 162 F.Supp.2d at 1181; Grosso v. Miramax Film Corp. (9th Cir. 2004) 383 F.3d 965; Merrill v. Paramount Pictures, Corp. (C.D. Cal. 2005) 78 U.S.P.Q.2d (BNA) 1192; Mestre v. Vivendi Universal US Holding Co. 2005 U.S. Dist. LEXIS 41024, *aff'd*. in unpublished opinion, 273 Fed. Appx 631 (9th Cir. 2008) ; *Benay* 607 F.3d at 625–626.

31. E.M. Forster, *Aspects of the Novel* (New York: Rosetta-Books, 2002). Story is "a narrative of events arranged in their time sequence. A plot is also a narrative of events, the emphasis falling on causality. 'The king died, and then the queen died,' is story. 'The king died, and then the queen died of grief' is plot" (pp. 23, 61).

32. Neil Landau with Matthew Frederick, *101 Things I Learned in Film School* (New York: Grand Central, 2010), p. 22.

33. Identity Arts v. Best Buy, 2007 U.S. Dist. LEXIS 32060

34. *Grosso,* 383 F.3d at 977 ("Both works have poker settings but the only similarities in dialogue between the two works come from the use of common, unprotectable poker jargon").

35. *Benay,* 607 F.3d at 628.

36. *Sony Pictures,* 156 F.Supp.2d at 1159.

37. *Mestre,* U.S. Dist. LEXIS 41024.

38. *Weygand,* 43 U.S.P.Q.2d (BNA) 1120; *Sony Pictures,* 156 F.Supp. 2d at 1148; Buggs v. Dreamworks, Inc., 2010 U.S. Dist. LEXIS 141515; Funky Films, Inc. v. Times Warner Entm't Co., L.P. (9th Cir. 2006) 462 F.3d 1072.

39. *Idema,* 162 F.Supp.2d at 1177–1178; Gable v. National Broadcasting Co. (C.D. Cal. 2010) 727 F.Supp.2d 815, 846–847; Bernal v. Paradigm Talent and Literary Agency (C.D. Cal. 2010) 788 F.Supp.2d 1043; *Benay,* 607 F.3d at 628.

40. Wild v. NBC Universal, Inc. (C.D. Cal. 2011) 788 F. Supp.2d 1083, *aff'd* in unpublished opinion, 513 Fed.Appx. 640.

41. *Mestre,* 2005 U.S. Dist. LEXIS 41024.

42. *Overman,* 605 F.Supp. at 352.

43. *Bernal,* 788 F.Supp.2d at 1070.

44. Benjamin v. Walt Disney Company, 2007 U.S. Dist. LEXIS 91710.

45. *Weygand,* 43 U.S.P.Q.2d (BNA) 1120; *Sony Pictures,* 156 F.Supp. 2d at 1148; *Buggs,* 2010 U.S. Dist. LEXIS 141515; *Funky Films,* 462 F.3d at 1072.

46. *Idema,* 162 F.Supp.2d at 1177–1178; *Gable,* 727 F.Supp.2d at 846–847; *Bernal,* 788 F.Supp.2d at 1070; *Benay,* 607 F.3d at 628.

47. DC Comics v. Towle (9th Cir. 2015) 802 F.3d 1012, 1019, citing Halicki Films, LLC v. Sanderson Sales and Marketing (9th Cir. 2008) 547 F.3d 1213, 1224.

48. Rice v. Fox Broadcasting Co. (9th Cir. 2003) 330 F.3d 1170, 1175, citing Toho Co., Ltd. v. William Morrow and Co., Inc. (C.D. Cal. 1998) 33 F.Supp.2d 1206, 1215.

49. Metro-Goldwyn-Mayer, Inc. v. American Honda Motor Co. (C.D. Cal. 1995) 900 F.Supp 1287, 1296 (James Bond is a protectable character under copyright).

50. Anderson v. Stallone (C.D. Cal. 1989) 11 U.S.P.Q.2d (BNA) 1161, 1165–1167 (Rocky is a protectable character under copyright).

51. *Toho,* 33 F.Supp.2d at 1215–1216 (Godzilla is a protectable character under copyright).

52. Sapon v. DC Comics (S.D.N.Y. 2002) 62 U.S.P.Q.2d (BNA) 1691, 1693–1694 (Batman is a protectable character under copyright).

53. *DC Comics,* 802 F.3d at 1019–1022 (the Batmobile is a protectable character under copyright).

54. *Jason,* 526 F.Supp. at 777 speaks in terms of "sequence" (see also *Overman,* 605 F.Supp. at 352). But starting with *Litchfield,* 736 F.2d at 1357, the element is referred to as "sequence of events."

55. *Berkic,* 761 F.2d at 1292.

56. *Jason,* 526 F.Supp. at 777.

57. *Overman,* 605 F.Supp. at 353; *Sony Pictures,* 156 F.Supp.2d at 1156–1157; *Idema,* 162 F.Supp.2d at 1177–1178.

58. *Shaw,* 919 F.2d at 1362; *Benay,* 607 F.3d at 628–629.

59. *Berkic,* 761 F.2d at 1294; Olson v. National Broadcasting Company, Inc. (9th Cir. 1988) 855 F.2d 1446, 1453; *Shaw,* 919 F.2d at 1353, 1357.

60. *Berkic,* supra, citing *Litchfield,* 736 F.2d at 1357.

61. *Krofft,* 562 F2d at 1172.

62. *Krofft,* supra; Fink v. Goodson-Todman Enterprises, Ltd. (1970) 9 Cal. App.3d 996, 1013.

63. See Fed. R. Civ. P. 8 (affirmative defenses).

64. 28 U.S.C. §§ 1331, 1338(a), 17 U.S.C. § 301.

65. 17 U.S.C. § 301(a); see also Briarpatch Ltd. v. Phoenix Pictures, Inc. (2nd Cir. 2004) 373 F.3d 296, 305, *cert. denied,* 554 U.S. 949, 125 S.Ct. 1704, 161 L.Ed.2d 525 (2005).

66. 28 U.S.C. § 1338(a).

67. *Grosso,* 383 F.3d at 967–978.

68. Using multiple theories of recovery—called "causes of action"—is a very typical situation and litigation strategy.

69. The trigger for invoking copyright subject matter jurisdiction under Title 17 U.S.C. § 102(a).

70. Cal. Code of Civ. Proc. § 339 (two-year statute of limitations for breach of oral contract in California).

71. 17 U.S.C. § 507(b) (three-year statute of limitations for copyright infringement).

72. Cal. Code of Civ. Proc. § 337 (four-year statute of limitations for breach of written contract in California).

73. Aalmuhammed v. Lee (9th Cir. 2000) 202 F.3d 1227, 1230–1231.

74. Houts v. Universal City Studios, Inc. (C.D. Cal. 1984) 603 F.Supp. 26, 28.

75. 17 U.S.C. § 507(b) (copyright statute of frauds).

76. Id.

77. Id.

CHAPTER SIX. YOUR LEGAL TEAM

1. Konigsberg Int'l, Inc. v. Rice (9th Cir. 1994) 16 F.3d 355.

2. Some examples of writers representing themselves without a lawyer and losing: Campbell v. The Walt Disney Company (N.D. Cal. 2010) 718 F.Supp.2d 1108; Quaglia v. Bravo Network, 2006 U.S. App. LEXIS 30995 (unpublished opinion); Flaherty v. Filardi (S.D.N.Y. 2005) 388 F.Supp.2d 274; Friedkin v. Double-U Productions, 2002 Cal. App. Unpub. LEXIS 10382; Kok v. Warner Bros., 2002 Cal. App. Unpub. LEXIS 8308; Whitehead v. Viacom (D.C. Md. 2002) 233 F.Supp.2d 715; Idema v. Dreamworks, Inc. (C.D. Cal. 2001) 162 F.Supp.2d 1129 (the plaintiffs filed the complaint without counsel and then ran into trouble and lost); Beal v. Paramount Pictures Corp. (11th Cir. 1994) 20 F.3d 454; Klekas v. EMI Films, Inc. (1984) 150 Cal. App.3d 1102.

3. Based on the book with the same title by Jonathan Harr.

4. Marisa Tomei won the Academy Award as for Best Actress in a Supporting Role for this performance. Art imitates life— the most persuasive witness is often the most expert witness.

5. Gable v. National Broadcasting Company (C.D. Cal. 2010) 727 F.Supp.2d 815, 834; citing Stewart v. Cachowiski (C.D. Cal. 2005) 574 F.Supp.2d 1074, 1106 n.130 (expert was an English professor who had previously testified in several matters regarding substantial similarity); West v. Perry 2009 U.S.Dist LEXIS 63422 (among other qualifications, expert had a film degree, was an accomplished screenwriter, and had worked as a screen credit arbitrator for the Writers Guild of America); A Slice of Pie Productions v. Wayans Bros. Entertainment (D.Conn. 2007) 487 F.Supp.2d 33, 41 (expert had extensive experience teaching, evaluating, studying, and writing about screen writing).

6. Instruction 2.11, "Expert Opinion," *Ninth Circuit Model Civil Jury Instructions,* www.akd.uscourts.gov/sites/akd/files/model_jury_civil.pdf.

7. Fed. R. Evid. 26(a)(2)(D).

8. Bernal v. Paradigm Talent and Literary Agency (C.D. Cal. 2010) 788 F.Supp.2d 1043, 1062 (expert witness "will 'seldom be necessary' to determine substantial similarity between literary works"); *Gable*, 727 F.Supp.2d at 836 (expert witness "only marginally helpful").

9. See *Gable*, supra, at 837 n. 18, citing Olson v. National Broadcasting Company, Inc. (9th Cir. 1988) 855 F.2d 1446, 1449; Sid & Marty Krofft Television Productions, Inc. v. McDonald's Corp. (9th Cir. 1977) 562 F.2d 1157, 1164.

10. Fed. R. Evid. 702.

11. Fed. R. Civ. P. 26(a)(2)(A).

12. Fed. R. Civ. P. 26(a)(2)(B).

13. Fed. R. Civ. P. 26(b)(4).

14. Fed. R. Civ. P. 26(b)(4)(A).

15. Fed. R. Civ. P. 26(b)(4)(E).

CHAPTER SEVEN. CONFESSIONS OF AN EXPERT WITNESS

1. Fed. R. Evid. 603. ("Before testifying, a witness must give an oath or affirmation to testify truthfully. It must be in a form designed to impress that duty on the witness's conscience.")

2. Buchwald v. Paramount Pictures Corp., 1990 Cal.App. LEXIS 634 (*Coming to America*).

3. See Pierce O'Donnell and Dennis McDougal, *Fatal Subtraction: The Inside Story of Buchwald v. Paramount* (New York: Doubleday, 1992).

4. Chase-Riboud v. DreamWorks, Inc. (C.D. Cal. 1997) 987 F.Supp. 1222 (*Amistad*).

5. Dunn v. Brown (D.C. Mass. 2007) 517 F.Supp.2d 541 (*The Da Vinci Code*).

6. Warner Bros. v. Film Ventures Int'l. (C.D. Cal. 1975) 403 F.Supp. 522 (*The Exorcist*).

7. Funky Films v. Time Warner Entertainment (9th Cir. 2006) 462 F.3d 1072 (*Six Feet Under*).

EPILOGUE: CREATIVITY AND COPYRIGHT

1. This is meant to be descriptive, not prescriptive. Having a spec "labor of love" project on the side can be a sanity touchstone for working writers.

APPENDIX A: COPYRIGHT FUNDAMENTALS

1. U.S. Const. art. I, § 8, clause 8 (emphasis added). Traditionally referred to as the Progress Clause, but now sometimes also called the Copyright Clause or the Patent Clause or the Intellectual Property Clause.

2. The Statute of Anne, also known as the Copyright Act 1710, 8 Ann. C. 21 (Parliament of Great Britain).

3. 17 U.S.C. § 101 et seq.

4. 17 U.S.C. § 106(1).

5. 17 U.S.C. § 106(3).

6. 17 U.S.C. § 106(2).

7. 17 U.S.C. § 106(4).

8. 17 U.S.C. § 502 et seq.

9. 17 U.S.C. § 501(a).

10. The Berne Convention Implementation Act of 1988, effective March 1, 1989.

11. 17 U.S.C. § 302(a) as amended by the 1998 Act.

12. H.R. Rep. No. 94-1476 regarding the 1998 copyright extension amendment to 17 U.S.C. § 302.

13. Act of May 31, 1790, ch. 15, § 1, 1 Stat. 124 (1790 Act).

14. Act of February 3, 1831, ch. 16, §§ 1, 16, 4 Stat. 436, 439 (1831 Act).

15. Act of March 4, 1909, ch. 320, §§ 23–24, 35 Stat. 1080–1081 (1909 Act).

16. See H.R. Rep. No. 94-1476, p. 135 (1976).

17. Eldred v. Ashcroft (2003) 537 U.S. 186; 123 S. Ct. 769; 154 L. Ed. 2d 683; U.S. Supreme Court rehearing denied by Eldred v. Ashcroft, 538 U.S. 916, 155 L.Ed. 2d 243, 123 S.Ct. 1505, 2004 U.S. LEXIS 2133 (2003).

18. 17 U.S.C. § 302(a) and (c).

19. Council Directive 93/98/EEC of 29 October 1993 Harmonizing the Term of Protection of Copyright and Certain Related Rights, 1993 Official J. Eur. Cmty. 290 (EU Council Directive 93/98).

20. 17 U.S.C. § 408(a).

21. 17 U.S.C. § 411(a).

22. 17 U.S.C. § 410(c).

23. 17 U.S.C. § 412, 504–505.

24. 17 U.S.C. § 410(d).

25. 17 U.S.C. § 410(a).

26. 17 U.S.C. § 201(a).

27. 17 U.S.C. § 101, "work made for hire" definition regarding motion pictures in paragraph (2); see also 17 U.S.C. § 201(b).

28. Cf. U.S.C. § 101, "work made for hire" definition regarding employees in paragraph (1).

29. Shaw v. Lindheim (9th Cir. 1990) 919 F.2d 1353, 1362.

30. Phillips v. Murdock (D.C. Hawaii 2008) 543 F.Supp.2d 1219, 1224–1225 (Copyright Office regulations state that "[w]ords and short phrases such as names, titles and slogans" are not subject to federal copyright protection; 37 C.F.R. § 202.1(a)).

31. See www.mpaa.org. See also Johnston v. Twentieth Century-Fox Film Corporation (1947) 82 Cal.App.2d 796, 804 (referencing registration through the Motion Picture Producers and Distributors of America, the predecessor of the MPAA).

32. Circ. 38A, "International Copyright Relations of the United States," www.copyright.gov/circs/circ38a.pdf.

APPENDIX B: COLLABORATION PROBLEMS

1. You don't necessarily need a lawyer to write the collaboration agreement for you. You're writers—express your intentions and expectations as clearly as you can. (See chapter 3, "Collaboration.") But it wouldn't hurt to have a lawyer give the collaboration agreement a quick review for you before you sign it.

2. Childress v. Taylor (2nd Cir. 1991) 945 F.2d 500, 508–509. But see *Nimmer on Copyright* § 6.07[A][3][a], at 22 (suggesting that each author's contribution need not be copyrightable). The key is the intent of the parties at the time the work is done.

3. Thomson v. Larson (2nd Cir. 1998) 147 F.3d 195, 201–202, citing *Childress*, 945 F.2d at 508.

4. *Nimmer on Copyright* § 6.03, at 7. Each author's contribution, however, must be more than de minimis. Id., § 6.07[A][1], at 21.

5. *Childress*, 945 F.2d at 508–509.

Index

Abstraction Test, 14
access, 55–57; burden of proving, 102; connection or nexus, 78; copyright infringement cases and, 77; defined, 77; substantial similarity and, 77, 96–97, 99–101; timing and, 77; tracing chain of intermediary persons, 78–80
Ace in the Hole (film, 1951, dir. Wilder), 58
advertising, 34, 138
Aeschylus, 16
agents, 23, 26, 54, 60; access to scripts and, 78–79, 80; as coauthors, 45; recognition of new writers and, 151–52; spec writers without, 52
All-Story magazine, 25
AMC, rebranding of, 16
Amistad (film, 1997), 137–38
Anderson, Paul Thomas, 33
Andromeda Strain, The (film, 1971), 23
antitrust settlement (1948), 64
appeals, legal, 70, 71, 84

Aristotle, 15
Aspects of the Novel (Forster), 87, 185n31
Austen, Jane, 27
authorship, 10, 108, 167, 175; "author" under copyright law, 168, 169; "original" works of, 159; WGA registration and, 166; "work made for hire" and, 169; writer's compensation tied to, 64. *See also* coauthorship

bargaining power, unequal, 61
Bass, Ron, 153
Beatlemania (musicians impersonating the Beatles), 145–47
Berkic v. Crichton (1985), 4
Berne Convention for the Protection of Literary and Artistic Works, 163, 171–72, 190n10
Bernheim, Alan, 135, 136, 137
Beverly Hills Bar Association, 117
billable hours, attorneys', 121–22

Marlowe, Christopher, 16
Medicine Man (film, 1992), 144–45
Melville, Herman, 27
merchandise, 34, 35, 75
"Mickey Mouse Protection Act"
(1998), 163
misconceptions, 30, 32, 33, 76, 145
Mitchell, Margaret, estate of, 170
mood, in substantial similarity
test, 89–90
Motion Picture Producers and
Distributors of America, 191n31
MPAA (Motion Picture Association of America), 170, 191n31
multinational corporations, as
copyright holders, 150
Murphy, Eddie, 135, 136, 137
music, 90, 145–47
Mutiny on the Amistad (Jones), 138
My Cousin Vinny (film, 1992), 124,
188n4

narrative, 22, 93
news, as true events, 5, 8–10, 14, 15,
84, 114
newspaper articles, 30
New York, 54, 59, 84, 175, 176. *See
also* Second Circuit Court of
Appeals
Ninth Circuit Court of Appeals
(California), 82, 98, 115, 147, 177;
copyright infringement cases,
69, 84; expert witnesses and, 129;
substantial similarity test of,
85–96, 184n28
non-disclosure agreements, 10–11,
63, 69, 83, 133
novels, acquisition of rights to,
26–27

options, buying, 28–29
oral agreements, 46, 181n7

Outbreak (film, 1995), 23
Overman v. Universal Studios, Inc.
(1984), 184n28
ownership, as prima facie element,
73–75

pace, in substantial similarity test,
90, 91
parallel development, 104–5
Paramount Pictures, 17, 57–58;
Coming to America case (1988), 135,
136, 137
partnership, collaboration and,
51–52
patronage: in premodern times,
1–2, 158; taxpayers as public
patrons, 8
permissions, 3, 21; life rights and,
32, 33; misconceptions about, 30;
risks of asking, 23–24
Pesci, Joe, 124
photocopying, 82
Picasso, Pablo, 18
pitching, 13, 66–67, 78; *Desny v.
Wilder* case and, 59, 182n5; of
ideas only, 64–65; leave-behinds
and, 65–66, 112; as "loss leader,"
63; protection of material
during, 3
pitch meetings, 11, 12, 112; implied
contract in, 59, 63; tracing access
to scripts and, 78
plagiarism, 30, 148, 160–61
plays, as "expressive works," 34–35
plots: limited number of, 30, 60; plot
in relation to story, 87, 185n31;
sequence of events and, 93; in
substantial similarity test, 86–87
"plus factor," in state court, 109
Polti, Georges, 30
Postal Service, United States,
166–67